MYSTERIES OF KNOWN UNKNOWNS

Tales of an African Dynasty

Book Two

Babatunde Olaniran

Mysteries of Known Unknowns: Tales of an African Dynasty
(Book Two)

First Printed in United Kingdom 2022

Published by Conscious Dreams Publishing
www.consciousdreamspublishing.com

Cover design by Jerry Wolf
Edited by Elise Abram and Karolyn Herrera
Typeset by Amit Dey

ISBN: 978-1-915522-19-1

**Gbogbo alángbá ló danú délè,
akó mo èyí tínú nrun.**

*   *   *

All lizards move with their stomachs facing the ground,
yet no one knows which one has an upset stomach.
In other words,

**People may appear to look the same,
yet the one with bad intentions may remain hidden.**

Contents

ONE

————◦••◦————

The skies began to grow dark, and the town of Ìkirè grew quiet after a very busy day. Most farmers were concluding the preparation of their land and getting ready to begin planting crops on their farms. Men and women wrapped up the day on their farms as soon as the sun began to set and went home to have dinner and spend time with their families. By eight every evening, Ìkirè town seemed like a ghost town. True to the popular saying, 'Early to bed, early to rise,' the young men and women who worked on farms preferred to go to bed early so they could set out again just before sunrise. As emphasized by the King of Ìkirè, focus was very important for achieving success in just about everything, and the farmers generally believed that the more focused they were, the less time they wasted, and the greater the productivity and output they achieved on their farmlands.

The only individuals found roaming around in Ìkirè Kingdom at that late hour were the *ode* (security men or vigilantes) and a few others who had remained a little longer on their farms. The kingdom was a particularly safe place during both the day and

1

at night. People travelling at such late hours were very careful to avoid the ode. These vigilante groups consisted of heavily armed men with little to no tolerance for misconduct. They carried various types of weapons and charms that caused the average citizen to fear them quite a bit. King Adéorí took the security of his people's lives and properties very seriously, and as such, he made sure the weapons for the *ode* were procured regularly. The vigilante groups were fully equipped and had recently had their arms updated by the King, who had traded some raw materials for more sophisticated weapons from a renowned weapons dealer in Britain. These newly acquired weapons were not common in the region and brought the ode increasing respect and fear both within and beyond the kingdom.

On the same evening, the Basòrun's family had just finished having dinner in their home, and the maid was clearing the short wooden table and cleaning up. As the family sat outside together under the moonlight to enjoy the serene evening, the Basòrun's wife excused herself to the kitchen to give some instructions to the family's three maids.

The Basòrun sat on a stool, sipping palm wine from his bowl. His two sons, Olúmólá and Oládélé, sat on either side of their father close to his feet, also sipping palm wine, and gazing into the darkness beneath the beautiful full moon. The stars glowed brightly, lighting up the magnificent night sky.

The Basòrun took another gulp from his bowl of wine, took a deep breath, and spoke to his sons: 'My sons, I am sure you both know that our family has been very prosperous for many centuries. Our farms are the largest across the kingdom. We have the largest workforce, second only to that of the King, that has come from within and outside of Ìkirè to work on our farms. Our family has also paid the most taxes to the palace for centuries without competition because no other family earns as much as we do in the entire kingdom.'

Olúmólá and Oládélé responded, '*Bééni bàá mi* (Yes, my father).'

The Basòrun nodded his head in affirmation and continued: 'We eat what we like when we like and how we like. We wear the best clothing materials, and as you both know, our family's lineage is known throughout the entire kingdom as holding the position of Basòrun, the second in command and the second most powerful family in the kingdom. Second only to the *adé* (crown).'

Both sons responded: 'This is true, very true, bàá mi.' Both young men had smiles on their faces knowing full well the importance of their family within and beyond the kingdom and the extent of the wealth they controlled.

'My sons, the only problem we have is that we are the *second* most powerful family, the *second* wealthiest family, and the *second* most important family. We are second in everything, and that is our problem. *Nkan tó bá kan ójú yí ò padà kan ímú* (Whatever affects the eye will eventually affect the nose). But it is not our problem alone. This has been a generational problem. It was the problem of our ancestors, and it will automatically become your problem as well, my sons, if I am not able to find a solution in my lifetime. If that is, unfortunately, the case, you must both make sure that you do all you can within your means to place our family in its rightful position where it belongs: the first family in this kingdom.'

3

Olúmólá's and his younger brother, Oládélé's, eyes met. Their father looked at both of them, one after the other, with a tough smile on his face as he patted both of them on their shoulders.

The Basòrun continued: 'We have been fighting a secret war for centuries. We either win or eventually become extinct one day. My father—your grandfather—told me he'd promised his father that he would do all he could to win this battle. *Èmi náà se àdéhùn fún bàbá mi wípé mà ná owó mà sí nà ára láti ri pé a borí* (I also promised my father that I would spend my money, my body, and everything within my power to see that we win this battle).' He paused to ask Olúmólá to pour him some more palm wine.

As Olúmólá picked up the jar of wine, Oládélé asked their father a very naïve but relevant question: '*Bàá mi* (My father)—who is this enemy with whom we are in a battle? Against whom are we fighting? You haven't told us, bàá mi. We need to know them so we can take them down anytime we may meet them.'

Sixteen-year-old Oládélé showed obvious signs of a boy who was growing into a strong, fearless man, most likely tougher than his older brother, but his naivety was evident from his question. Nonetheless, his father had a broad smile on his face because, in the midst of his son's inexperience, he heard the passion and intensity to fight in Oládélé's voice.

The Basòrun responded: 'Oládélé, you are a true son of your father. The enemy with whom we are in battle is very strong. Remember, our ancestors have been in this battle for centuries without winning. The answer will gradually become clearer to you as you grow older, but for now, I want you to know that any family or person in the way of our family's becoming the first family is an enemy, and that includes the family presently ruling this kingdom. What this means is, indirectly, we will have lots of enemies. We will need to convert some of them to friends because we will need them on our side. Likewise, we will be forced to eliminate others to allow us our space and room to breathe.'

At this, both boys were confused, but they knew they could trust their father, and they nodded their heads in acceptance.

'Bàá mi,' said Olúmólá. 'We promise you that we will do everything in our capacity to win this battle.' He looked at his brother Oládélé, who nodded in agreement.

'Great. We have gotten closer to our goal over the years, and we couldn't be closer than we are now. Remember that your sister, Olúfúnké, is now the queen of this kingdom, and she is the one who will bear the heir to the throne.

'That will be all for tonight, my sons. I will keep you both informed as our strategic plan progresses. I know we will win this battle together. You may now go to bed for the night.'

'Thank you, bàá mi,' Olúmólá and Oládélé said to their father.

The Basòrun's sons got up from their seated position next to their father and proceeded to their rooms for the night.

Chief Oláòsebìkan, the Basòrun, spent some time alone in the yard after the boys went in. His mind wandered in different directions. The thought of his daughter and the day she would bear the heir to the throne of Ikire Kingdom made him smile. Memories of his late father flashed through his mind. He wondered what his father would have thought about his current approach to achieving the goal of reaching the throne. '*Ó dá mi lójú wípé inú bàbá mi yí ò dùn* (I am sure my father would be happy),' he said out loud.

He picked up a kolanut from the clay tray in front of him, bit into it, and said a prayer to his ancestors for guidance and protection. He then poured more wine and made a toast to his ancestors, smiling. It was now a few minutes past nine, and the moonlight shone brightly over the compound. With a renewed feeling of hope and fulfilment, Chief Oláòsebìkan stood up from his wooden chair, looked up at the sky, and reiterated, 'I promised you, bàá mi, and I will accomplish my promise to you.'

TWO

---·I·---

On December 3, 1899, the cocks blessed the early hours of the morning with their first calls of the day. Everything else was quiet aside from the cocks crowing at intervals and the usual cooing sounds of the palm doves. King Adéorí's chambers were heavily guarded but as quiet and as peaceful as a graveyard. Since Adéorí's early teen years, waking up to the first cock crow in the morning had been the norm. Unsurprisingly, his body had become accustomed to this over the years. As he opened his eyes, he remembered that his late father used to tell him that wise men rose with the sound of the first cock crow of the day. *This meant I must have been a wise man, even when I was a young boy*, he thought.

With a full stretch and a smile, he arose out of his beautiful palatial bed and walked towards the golden sculptures of his ancestors that stood on the other side of his room as he did first thing every morning.

Adéorí knelt down in front of the sculptures and lifted his hands to the sky to say a prayer.

'*Mo jú bà Olódùmarè* (I salute you, oh, Lord). *Mo jú bà a sè èdá ayé* (I salute you, the creator of the world). *Mo jú bà Olórun mí àti Olórun àwon baba mi* (I salute you, my lord and the lord of my forefathers), *eni tí ń so òru dì árò* (the one that turns the night into the day). *Mo jú bà àwon Irúnmolè* (I salute the deities of our land). *Esé tí e jí mi sí orí lè ayé léní yí* (Thank you for waking me up on the earth today); *kìí se mímò mi, esé o* (it's not of my own doing, thank you).' Adéorí got up from his kneeling position and walked to the washroom.

Every morning, he awoke at the same time, said the same prayers, and followed the same routine. His stomach felt a little upset as he approached the washroom, but he didn't think it was anything he should worry about. He used the facilities and prepared to take a bath. As he took his bath, he wondered why the sound of the crowing cock was heavier than usual that morning. Was it the same cock that crowed that morning as on every other morning? There had been something strange about it, and he felt like that morning's crow was trying to wake him up to something different. As he continued to wash, he thought *Ìfura nì ògùn àgbà* (The greatest weapon of the elders is suspicion).

Shaking off the awkward thoughts about the crowing cock, he spent another fifteen minutes washing before stepping back into his room.

As he dried off, a spark of lightning flashed through the windows of his room, and a loud crash of thunder followed, striking the skies and shaking the entire room. Everything moved, and his father's sculpture—one among those he had knelt in front of earlier to say a prayer—fell off its pedestal. '*Èwò* (Abomination)!' he exclaimed as he moved quickly to pick up the sculpture. While

Adéorí moved his father's sculpture back into its proper position, he chanted, '*Oba nígbà ayé, Oba lójú orun* (A king while on earth and a king in death). *Oba kìí subú bí ó wà láyé àbí kò sí láyé* (A king doesn't fall whether he is alive or dead).'

While repositioning his late father's golden sculpture, rain began pouring heavily from the skies. The awkward cock crow and the series of events that followed led Adéorí to become even more suspicious. His whole being indicated that something was wrong, but he could not imagine or put a finger on what it could be. King Adéorí shrugged off these troubled thoughts once more, and as the rain continued to pour down, he dressed and went into his study to begin making plans for the day.

At a quarter past nine that same morning, King Adéorí heard a knock on his chamber's outer door. He was sitting in his study, planning and preparing for an upcoming meeting with a few monarchs from the Yorùbá land and some British businessmen who would be representing the interests of a British company. The Oòni of Ifè had called for the meeting, which had been scheduled for a fortnight in Ifè Kingdom. The outcome of the meeting had the potential to bring tremendous economic advantages and development to the entirety of the Yorùbá land. Aside from King Adéorí, the Oòni of Ifè also invited the Aláàfin of Òyó, Oba of Benin, the Awùjalè of Ìjèbú, and the Aláké of Ègbá Land to the meeting. These monarchs controlled vast kingdoms. They were the wealthiest and most influential amongst monarchs in the Yorùbá land. The Oòni had asked King Adéorí to join them because of his proven business acumen and ability to successfully negotiate very profitable deals with the British.

The knocking continued, resonating harder on the King's door. Obviously, only one of the queens could have gone past the guards in his chambers without being stopped or questioned.

'*Wo lé o* (Come in),' he called. Queen Adéòsun, his first wife, opened the door and walked in. She went through the King's room into the study, where she found him sitting and working.

'*Ekú àárò, Oko mí* (Good morning, my husband),' she said, kneeling down close to his chair.

King Adéorí responded with a smile, '*Kù àárò aya mí, aya oba* (Good morning, my wife, the wife of the King).' The King was fond of addressing each queen as 'the wife of the King'. '*Sé dada lo jí* (I hope you woke up well)?' he asked as he pulled Adéòsun up from her kneeling position so she could sit on the stool beside him.

'*Bééni Oko mí, Orun alááfia ni mo sùn* (Yes, my King. My sleep was peaceful),' answered the queen. 'I am surprised to see that you are hard at work already, my lord. I inquired of the guards outside, and they confirmed you have not been out of your room yet this morning. You seem pretty busy, my lord.'

'Yes, Olorì,' said the King. 'I received a message from the Oòni last week for an upcoming meeting at his palace. It is an important meeting, and I have a few things to prepare, so it goes as planned. I have a very tight schedule for the next few weeks, so the earlier I complete preparations for the meeting, the better.'

Queen Adéòsun nodded her head in confirmation.

'What has brought you here to me this morning, my Queen?' asked Adéorí. 'Is everything okay? Did you see me in your dream, or have you just come to say hello and check on me as you always do?' They both laughed at the King's question.

'I came here to check on you, my King, per usual,' replied Queen Adéòsun. 'Something has also been bothering me for a few days now, and I have come to discuss it with you, Your Majesty.'

'Sé ò sí (I hope there is no problem),' he said with concern.

'I do not know if there is a problem, my King, but I have come to discuss it with you as soon as possible so that even if it were a problem, it could easily be resolved.'

The King wondered what this was all about, and he suddenly remembered the strange feelings he'd experienced all morning since he'd awoken. 'I am all ears, Olorí. Speak to me.'

'Lénu ojò mèta (For the past three days),' began the Queen, 'I have noticed something strange happening in the palace, my King. I saw Queen Adénìké two days ago, and when I opened up a conversation with her, I noticed she was in a rush to leave my presence. At the time, I assumed this was her usual attitude or that she had things to take care of that required her urgent attention. Yesterday evening, I went to visit her in her chambers to discuss some of the new developments and plans to empower and train a new set of young ladies who had recently been admitted to our foundation. Upon arriving at her chambers, her guards and maidens would not permit me to enter. I figured she had ordered them not to permit anyone into her chambers until she was first informed. However, this order was to prevent anyone from entering into her chambers under any circumstance, my lord,' she lamented. 'Of course, she has every right to give her direct staff such an order, but she should have informed them to make some exceptions to such an order. Unfortunately for her, the guards could not stop me, so I went into her chambers and waited for her to come out of her inner chambers into the common room.'

Queen Adéòsun paused for a moment to catch her breath before she continued: 'As soon as Adénìké came out, I asked her why she had done that, and to my surprise, she immediately apologized and told me that the guards had misinterpreted her orders. She said she had not been feeling too well and needed some quiet time to herself. Not even two minutes into our conversation, she excused herself. She moved as quickly as she could to her inner chambers and was gone for at least five minutes. I could hear her clearing her throat, and after a little while, I heard the sound of water droplets. Obviously, she had been to the restroom. Shortly afterwards, she came out, and her face appeared heavy and swollen. Apart from that, she could barely speak to me, and I knew something was wrong. In fact, I could sense what the problem was. I advised that she try to get some rest and that I would speak to her when she is feeling better. Then, I took my leave.'

After listening to the older queen's account, King Adéorí wondered what could be wrong with Adénìké. He knew Adéòsun would not come to him to discuss things she had not seen. He thought for a moment before posing a question to her: 'Did you ask one of her guards or yours to fetch the herbal medicine man to check her out so he could find out exactly what is wrong and know what to prescribe for her?'

'No, my King. I did not do that,' replied the Queen. '*Nkan tó n se Adénìké jù béèlo* (What is wrong with Adénìké is more than that). I don't think a herbal medicine man can cure her problem.'

The King's face lit up. 'What do you mean?' he demanded, with a hint of authority in his tone.

'My King, I think Adénìkè is pregnant,' she said, smiling.

King Adéorí could not believe his ears. Like a swinging pendulum, Adéòsun's words resounded in his head multiple times, and he didn't know what to think. 'Are you sure about this, Olorì? You know this is very serious.'

'Yes, Your Majesty,' answered Adéòsun. 'I can tell when a woman is pregnant. Adénìké is showing all the signs, and when she ran into her room in my presence, I am certain she went to vomit.'

The King was speechless. He did not know how to respond. The news and how it was broken to him felt unusual. *This is good news*, he thought again. King Adéorí tried to remember the last time he had slept with Adénìké. 'Almost three months now, if I am not mistaken,' he wondered quietly to himself. Activities towards the end of last year's harvest season had kept him busy, and then came the impromptu sacrifice with Olúfúnké, which had obviously upset Adénìké. It had been barely a week since Queen Adénìké began visiting the King's chambers again, and they hadn't had any intimate physical contact. Could she possibly have been pregnant long before without knowing? So much was going on in his mind that he began to feel as if he could not hold the thoughts to himself. He got up from his chair and paced around his study for several minutes before speaking again.

'If what you are saying is correct, Olorì, this is good news for our kingdom. I will summon the traditional healer to visit Adénìké so they can confirm for us what exactly is going on before we get too excited.'

'Yes, my King. That is a great idea,' said the Queen. 'I will take my leave now. That is all I came to discuss with you, my lord.'

'Thank you, Olorì mi. I appreciate your support and concern. May the gods of our land and my ancestors bless you for being the mother of my palace,' said Adéorí.

'*Àse Olúwa mi* (Thank you, my lord),' Adéòsun responded. She got up from the stool, approached the door, and left the King's presence quietly.

Adéorí watched Olorì Adéòsun as she walked out of his study. He wasn't sure what to think about what he'd just heard. 'Could this be true?' he asked out loud. He thought about the new Queen Olúfúnké and remembered how he'd married her, the council meeting, the sacrifice and all the events that had happened at the time—could Adéníké have been pregnant *before* these events? What a blunder that would be. *But the gods never make mistakes*, he reminded himself. Once again, he tried to remember the last time he'd slept with Adéníké. It had been just about three months, and he knew for sure he hadn't mistaken the time.

After a few more minutes of deliberating over what might have happened, he decided that the best option would be to visit Adéníké himself to find out exactly what was going on. Hearing the news from her would dispel any doubt or speculation.

As soon as Adéorí rose from his chair, he heard another knock on the door.

'My lord?' This time it was one of his personal chamber guards.

'Come in,' King Adéorí instructed.

The guard entered almost immediately and prostrated himself as he greeted the King.

'*Kábíyèsí o, (He who cannot be questioned)*' said the chamber guard while remaining in the prostrated position for the King to respond to him.

'*O seun* (Thank you). You may now rise.'

The guard got up from his position and proceeded with the message he'd come to deliver: 'My lord, the high priest of Ìkirè is here to see you. He is waiting in the visitors' room, my lord.'

King Adéorí looked a little surprised as he was sure he had not scheduled an appointment with the high priest. Neither had he asked for the high priest to see him. 'Very well. Tell him I will be with him shortly. Arrange for some kolanuts and wine to be served while he waits for me.'

'Of course, my lord. Kábíyèsí o,' replied the palace guard before leaving the presence of the King.

There must be something distinctive about today, Adéorí thought. He finished making himself presentable for visitors, and after about twenty minutes, he stepped out of the inner room into his visitors' area to see the high priest.

King Adéorí was dressed in all-white regalia. His *agbádá* (long flowing robe with wide sleeves), *sòkòtò* (trousers), and cap fit him perfectly, and he looked twenty years younger than he truly was. He came in holding his golden staff in his right hand. The common tradition was for one of the personal guards to carry a staff when around the King within and outside the kingdom, but this particular golden staff was one the King carried, representing the ultimate sign of authority. The staff signified command, authority, and respect. It was widely believed that anything the King said while pointing the golden staff in the direction of the heavens became a command and shall come to pass. King Adéorí only exited his private chambers with the staff when something important was to be said or done or on days when his gut feeling didn't seem right, and that day was surely one of those days.

As the King walked into the large visitors' room, the guards and high priest immediately noticed the staff. The guards fell to their knees with their heads bowed as they repeated the phrase, 'Kábíyésí o,' continuously.

The high priest stood and bowed his head as the King walked towards his throne.

'Good morning, *agbenu òrìsà ńlá* (mouthpiece of the gods). Our people say that when the gods visit very early in the morning without notice, it means they have brought a warning—what brings you to my palace this morning unannounced and without a prior appointment?' asked King Adéorí.

'Good morning, Your Majesty, the King of our great kingdom,' replied the high priest. 'Thank you for receiving me without prior notice, my lord. *Àwon èyàn wa so wípé tí àgbàlagbà bá rí nkan tó ru lójú, ojú náà ni á fín wò se* (Our people say that if an elder sees something that is unpleasant, it is the same eyes he will use to see it in order to amend it). As you know, Your Majesty, I have an obligation to our land, and that, in turn, means I am a direct servant of *orí adé* (the crown). If we cannot be observant, pay attention, and heed warning signs, calamities will visit us at our doorsteps before we notice. May Olódùmarè, the gods of our land, and our ancestors do not allow calamities to reach our doorsteps before we see them approaching.' He paused as the King nodded mildly in acceptance.

'My King, I had a dream in the early hours of this morning, and I have been directed by the gods to bring a message to the palace. As you know, my lord, when a dream comes during a nap in the wee hours of the morning, it is important that we heed and pay close attention to it. As soon as I woke up from this dream, I got up to consult Ifá, and a few things were revealed to me. If you remember, Your Majesty, during our consultations with Ifá for a solution to the problem of an heir in the palace, Ifá revealed to us and gave us an *ìkìlò* (warning). This warning was that the palace, specifically our King, would receive unpleasant news about seven weeks after the sacrifice. Ifá also told us that Your Majesty would have to accept the news in good faith without getting angry, no matter how unpleasant the news was.'

King Adéorí nodded his head once again, confirming that he remembered the warning from Ifá.

'In my dream, your Majesty,' continued the high priest, 'I cannot say for sure what exactly happened, but one of the palace guards came to give me the message that you wanted my immediate attention at the palace. Upon arriving at the palace, I heard you speaking in a very loud voice, one loud enough to bring down the palace structure, but the words were not clear enough for me to understand what was being said. I heard you from outside your chambers and decided to go in. As I walked in, I noticed something unusual: no guards were present, and I wondered in the dream where all the guards had gone to. I walked into this same room we are sitting in presently and found no one but saw blood stains all over the floor and walls. The loud sound of your voice had faded away, and everything was silent. It was a horrific scene, but just before I could figure out what had happened, I awoke back to reality.'

King Adéorí couldn't stop shaking his head as he listened to the high priest's narrative. He had been nursing a very strange feeling all morning, one he could not understand, but one that was strong enough for him to know something wasn't right. He had not fully digested the news Olorì Adéòsun had brought to him before the high priest arrived, bringing a new dimension to the morning. He was unsure whether he should treat these occurrences individually or as interrelated and in a holistic manner. Intuition told him there must be a connection. The voice of his late father suddenly rang in his mind, reminding him of a phrase that had often been preached to him as a teenage boy: *Agbára sùúrù kò sé fi ojú di nígbà ìsoro* (The power of patience can never be underestimated in times of crisis and confusion). He affirmed these words to himself and told his inner consciousness that he would not make any decisions or conclusions in haste.

After about three minutes of absolute silence in the room, the King spoke: 'Thank you, high priest of our great kingdom. Thank you for continuously making the palace and our kingdom your top priority. I have heard all you have said, and we will pay heed to it. I cannot fathom what this predicament that is expected to greatly upset me will be. Even if I am told not to get angry over it, I know we are made and prepared to prevail over all types of circumstances. I will be here, waiting for whatever it is. Thank you again, high priest of our land. Is that all you have for me today?'

'Yes, your Majesty,' the high priest responded. 'Ifá directed me to bring this message to you first thing this morning. I will return to the shrine now, my lord. Kábíyèsí o.' He got up and showed his respect by bowing before the King before walking out of the visitors' room.

The morning had been an interesting one for the King, to say the least. His mind was now occupied with all manner of considerations. The thought that Olorì Adénìké could be carrying a child that was not his wasn't one he was willing to entertain. The King called the attention of one of his personal guards, Àlàbí, to give him certain directives. He then set out to Adénìké's chambers as he had initially planned before the high priest's visit to find out from her what was truly going on.

Meanwhile, Queen Adéòsun had gone directly to the chambers of Olúfúnké, the youngest Olorì, after she'd left the King. The young Olorì, who has now fully settled into palace life, was making herself some breakfast when one of her maidens informed her of the older queen's presence.

Recently, the older queens, Adéòsun and Adénìké, had requested their maidens prepare the daily meals, and they only made their own meals once or twice a week. When they were initially married to the King, they had prepared meals for themselves and the King daily. Olúfúnké was a great cook, and she made her own meals as she had at the house of her father, the Basòrun. As the new wife, she prepared the King's meals, and he loved this because she cooked so well. King Adéorí never failed to tell her how wonderful her food tasted and that her meals were some of the best he'd ever had.

Upon learning about Queen Adéòsun's arrival, Olúfúnké asked the maiden, who was helping her in her kitchen, to keep watching over the *èwà àti isu dídín* (beans and fried yam) she was making while she went to see Queen Adéòsun.

'*Ekáarò Olorì àgbà* (Good morning, older queen),' greeted Queen Olúfúnké.

Queen Adéòsun was sitting on a stool in the garden area in front of Olúfúnké's chambers. 'Good morning, my dear,' she answered with a smile. 'How are you doing this morning?'

Olúfúnké replied, 'I am fine, ma. I hope I did not keep you waiting too long. I was in the kitchen making breakfast.'

'That's fine, Olúfúnké. You are looking very bright and pretty this morning, as always,' said Adéòsun. 'You will have to share some of your beauty secrets with me so I can look as beautiful as you,' the older queen joked.

'Haaa Olorì àgbà!' exclaimed the younger queen. 'Esé (Thank you).' She blushed. 'We learned this from you. You imbibed the knowledge and beauty secrets people like myself take advantage of today.'

'Fair enough, and well said,' Queen Adéòsun responded. 'I hope you are in contact with your family and that they are all doing well.'

'Yes, my Queen. Everyone is fine. I see my father when he comes here to the palace to visit the King. He makes it a point of duty to see me before he leaves.'

'Marvelous,' Queen Adéòsun responded. 'I know you are a very nice lady. My prayer and hope are that we hear the cry of a baby from you in this kingdom very soon.'

'Ní agbára olódùmarè olorì àgbà (By the grace of the almighty, older queen),' said Olúfúnké. 'It is an interesting coincidence that you said that, olorì àgbà, because I asked one of the maidens to fetch me Ìyá alágbo not very long ago. I have been feeling very tired lately, àtipé miò tì rí ńkàn osù mi (and I haven't seen my period). Óse é se pé mo ti férakù (It is possible that I am pregnant).

You are like a mother to me, olorì àgbà, and I can hide nothing from you.'

Queen Adéòsun jumped up from the stool on which she was sitting in excitement. '*Ayò mí tidé o* (My joy is here)!' she cried. 'This is great news for everyone and the entire kingdom. Have you told the King about this yet?'

'No, I have not told the King yet. I want to make sure I have properly confirmed the news before mentioning it to him. I am also a little nervous about telling him.'

'No, please don't be nervous. There is absolutely nothing to be nervous about, my dear. The King will be extremely happy. This will bring him absolute and infinite joy. *Osé aya mi* (Thank you, my wife). Please keep me informed. Send a message to me immediately once Ìyá alágbo confirms. *Inú mi dùn ayò mí kún* (I am so happy and full of joy),' Adéòsun declared.

Queen Olúfúnké was very happy about the older queen's response to the news. 'Thank you, my Queen, and thank you for the support, ma,' she said, beaming.

The older queen got up to take her leave. She danced as she walked out of Olùfùnkè's chambers. Just before stepping out of the garden, she turned around. Olúfúnké was walking slowly behind her. 'You know,' Adéòsun said, 'I saw Queen Adénìké earlier this morning. I think she is pregnant, too. Although she did not confide in me as you did, my gut feeling tells me she is.'

Olúfúnké's face lit up when she heard these words from the older queen. Before she could say anything in response, Adéòsun added, 'My only worry is that I am not sure whether her pregnancy would bring the palace as good news as yours.'

Before Olúfúnké had time to make any sense of what Adéòsun had said, the older queen walked away. Olúfúnké's tongue felt locked in place, and her shock from what she had just heard kept her rooted in the same position, unable to move even a strand of hair. 'Why would Queen Adénìké's pregnancy *not* be a source of good news for the palace?' she wondered out loud.

She abruptly remembered she'd been cooking before the olorì àbgà had visited, and she rushed back into her chambers to the kitchen to finish up. As she continued throughout the morning, the older queen's words kept revisiting her thoughts even though she truly didn't know what to make of them.

THREE

———◦i◦———

L ater in the early afternoon, activities within the palace had begun for the day. Earlier, Oláolú had led a group of two hundred servants to a section of the more than one thousand hectares of land owned by the palace to complete the last phase of the land clearing and preparation. Oláolú usually directed the servants, accompanied by a group of twenty-five of the King's armed guards, who were assigned the duty of monitoring the servants' activities on the farm. Oláolú's job was to demarcate the land area and assign tasks to the other servants, as well as monitor the ongoing farm work. Although he headed the servants, he was under close supervision of the deputy controller of the King's guards, Àjàlá, who was in charge of the team of armed guards. The servants were divided into two groups, and they worked at intervals according to a timetable. Both were led by Oláolú. A sizeable number of servants had been left behind at the palace, performing other maintenance-related duties. Trees had shed their leaves all over the grounds, and some portions of the palace compound area were wet and flooded because of the recent heavy rainfall.

King Adéorí, escorted by five personal guards, set out from his chambers to see Queen Adénìké. Before leaving his chambers, he had breakfast, but he barely ate due to the contradicting thoughts oscillating back and forth in his head. Thoughts that Adénìké could be pregnant worried him, and the likelihood the pregnancy wasn't his worried him far more. *Is it even possible the pregnancy isn't mine?* Adéorí wondered as he walked across the palace field towards Adénìké's chambers.

The King was confident, and he trusted Adénìké, but from his vast experience, he also knew that the heart of man is deeper than can be imagined, and no one is above misdeeds. Adénìké was the only person to shed proper light on the situation to help him understand what exactly was going on. '*A kìì fá orí léyìn olórí* (We can't shave a head in the absence of the owner),' he said to himself.

As he approached the Queen's chambers, servants and maidens echoed 'Kábíyèsí o' from far and near, and King Adéorí waved his golden staff towards them as a sign of acknowledgement.

Upon arriving, the guards accompanying the King stopped in front as they always did anytime he visited any of his queens. The King walked into the garden area preceding the entrance to the chambers and was met by two of Queen Adénìké's maidens, who dropped to their knees as soon as they saw the King.

'Kábíyèsí o,' said both maidens.

Adéorí walked into the chambers' living area and found another maiden busy cleaning the area. 'Kábíyèsí o,' she said as she dropped to her knees to greet the King, her head facing the ground.

'Thank you. Where is my wife?' the King demanded.

The maiden remained in her kneeling position, and without looking up, responded, 'My Queen is in the inner chambers, my lord.'

'Go and inform her I am here,' Adéorí commanded.

She rose and proceeded to inform the queen of the King's presence. For the King to visit his queens in their chambers was not anything new, but it only happened once in a blue moon; it seemed as if there was a blue moon in the sky that day.

King Adéorí had much on his mind as he paced the large living area as if he were there to examine the entire living area as well as the wooden decorations in the room. Shortly after the maiden had left, she came back to notify the King that Queen Adénìké would be with him as soon as possible.

A few minutes afterwards, Queen Adénìké entered the living area, wearing an elegant white dress with a white head tie. She was surprised to see him, and she tried to hide her worry as much as she could. Once she'd received the message of the King's presence, she'd wondered why he decided to come to see her himself and not send one of his personal guards to ask her to visit him as he usually did. *It must be important*, she told herself as she hurried to get ready to meet him.

As she stepped into the living area, Adénìké found the King staring at one of the pieces of artwork displayed on the wall. She walked towards him and knelt down beside him. '*Ekáàsán oko mí* (Good afternoon, my husband).'

King Adéorí turned around to focus his attention on Adénìké, who was still on her knees and holding onto the King's agábádá.

She continued, '*Olólùfé mi, okoò mi, olówó orí mi* (My lover, my husband, and the owner of my dowry). It is unusual for you to come to my chambers. I hope everything is good, my lord?' she asked, remaining on her knees, worry coursing through every bone in her body.

King Adéorí replied, '*Kó má bà sí ni o fi rí mi olorì Adénìké* (It is so no problems will arise, that is why I am here, Queen Adénìké).'

The Queen noted that the King rarely called her Olori Adénìké.

'Please, get up,' he requested. Adéorí continued to pace in slower steps around the living area. 'Adénìké, are you pregnant?' he finally asked.

The King's question came as a shock to Adénìké and was the last thing she expected to hear. She felt as though she'd received an unexpected slap to the face. Before she took the time to think about her response, she said with a look of bewilderment, '*Rárá o olówó orí mi* (Not at all, my husband).

'Pregnancy? Maybe I am pregnant and don't know, my King, but that is definitely not something I know about. To get pregnant and bring a child into the palace would make me the happiest woman in the world. *Oko mí* (My husband), what sparked this question?' she asked.

King Adéorí felt relief and doubt at the same time. He had been paying close attention to every word that came out of Adénìké's mouth. He stared directly into her eyes as though the true answers to his questions lay within. Surely, he was no expert in the field, and he could in no way base his conclusion on something that might as well have been mere speculation by Adéòsun.

'Word came to me that you have not been feeling very well,' said the King. 'My initial intuition was that you could be pregnant, but of course, that would be wishful thinking on my part.' He smiled faintly. 'So, I decided to come to see you for myself to find out what is going on. How are you feeling? Do you feel ill in any way?'

At the King's response, Adénìké felt as though she'd been carrying something heavy on her head and had just been relieved of some of the weight. 'You are a very kind man, my love,' the Queen said, moving closer to her husband and hugging him tightly. Holding him gave her extra comfort from the anxiety and fear that had engulfed her since she'd first heard of his presence. She summoned the courage to look into his eyes as she held on to him.

'I am very happy you came here to see me, my great husband. Your kindness and love mean everything to me. I came down with a fever during the last three days, but I am feeling better now. I sent for Ìyá alágbo as soon as I began feeling these symptoms, and she visited immediately. One of the maidens brought me a herbal concoction she'd made for me. I have been taking it, and I'm feeling better now, my lord.'

'Okay, my sweet Adénìké,' said King Adéorí. 'I am glad you feel better now. I will ask my medicine man, Ifálóyé, to send someone to examine you again later today or tomorrow morning. We need to make sure that whatever is wrong with you has been properly taken care of, and we also need to be sure whether you are pregnant or not,' he said with a smile.

'Of course, you know I will be the happiest man in the world if you *are* pregnant.'

Queen Adénìké smiled back at her husband. She knew that the Queen who carried the King's baby would automatically be a paragon in all eyes and viewed in a different light within the palace. Of course, she wished to be the one to bear the next ruler of the kingdom, but being pregnant by someone else who was *not* the King but a palace servant would attract the absolute wrath of the King. How did he know or suspect she could be pregnant? Could olorì àgbà have gone to tell him this? She thought about the matter while hugging the King.

He patted her on the back gently for a few seconds before speaking again: 'My darling, Dénìké. I will have to take my leave now to attend to some pressing issues. As I mentioned earlier, Ifálóyé will visit you or send his people for further examination of your condition. Please let me know if you want or need anything as soon as the need arises. Come to my chambers later this evening also, so we can spend some more time together.'

'Thank you, my husband,' replied the Queen. 'I will come to the chambers this evening. Thank you for coming here. This means so much to me.' She relaxed her grip on the King, and he kissed her on the forehead before proceeding out of the living area. Adénìké walked with her husband to the door and hugged him again before he left.

Knowing her to be a very affectionate and loving soul, the King would not have any reason to think Adénìké's hugging and touching were out of place. Adénìké took a deep breath and went back into her inner chambers as soon as he'd left. Knowing full well that she had told the King the biggest lie any woman could tell her husband, she knelt down beside her bed and began to cry uncontrollably. She had cheated, gotten pregnant as a result, and lied to cover her actions, but she was also determined to keep all secrets to herself.

After crying for about fifteen minutes, she got up from her kneeling position and lay face down on the bed. *This has by far been the biggest test and threat to my existence*, she thought. As she continued to sob away, she vowed never to allow lust or emotions to override making the right decision to the extent of putting her in such a position ever again.

Contradicting thoughts filled King Adéorí's head as he walked back from Adenike's chambers. He wanted to believe everything Olorì Adénìké had told him, but for some unknown reason, he wasn't totally convinced. He had asked Àlàbí, one of his personal guards, to fetch Ifálóyé, the medicine man, and ask him to visit the palace urgently. Ifálóyé had been the King's medicine man for decades and was well-trusted. Adéorí knew that if Adénìké were truly pregnant and had told him a lie, Ifálóyé would detect the truth even though he secretly wished this wasn't the case. Something just didn't feel right at all. Throughout his life and time as a king, that day was one of the most awkward days he had encountered.

After settling back into his private chambers, he thought about Adéòsun's visit again and wondered why she'd been so certain that Adénìké was pregnant. Adéorí knew both queens disagreed frequently, and more often than not, would be on different sides of an issue, but he also knew that both women had a good conscience and put the palace first before anything else. Twenty minutes into his thoughts, the King heard a knock on the door.

'*Wolé* (Come in),' he instructed.

Àlàbí, the King's personal guard who had gone to fetch Ifálóyé, the medicine man, walked in and prostrated before him. 'Kábíyèsí o.'

'*O káre, Àlàbí. Gbé ra ńlè* (Well done, Àlàbí. Get up),' said King Adéorí.

'Thank you, my lord. Bàbá Ifálóyé is here, waiting for Your Majesty in the visitors' area.'

'Tell him I will be with him shortly,' said the King.

'Kábíyèsí o,' Àlàbí replied as he withdrew from the King's private chambers.

Just before Àlàbí stepped out the door, the King called out to him once more: 'Lest I forget, Àlàbí, go to olorì Adénìké's chambers right away and tell her to see me immediately.'

'Done, Your Majesty,' Àlàbí said, and he shut the door behind him. King Adéorí donned his crown, picked up his golden staff, and headed for the visitors' area to meet with Ifálóyé.

Ifálóyé was waiting patiently in the palace's visitors' area. Arguably one of the best medicine men and healers of his time, he was also known as a firm supporter of and loyalist to the King. King Adéorí only called on him when he had a duty for him, and he always performed diligently. But on that day, he wondered why the King required his immediate attention at the palace without any prior notice. It was unusual, but of course, when the King's call is heard, all must answer. While Ifálóyé waited for him, he noticed new pictures and sculptures had recently been placed on the walls, and he took some time to appreciate the beauty of the artwork.

While the medicine man was examining some of the beautiful art on the walls, King Adéorí walked into the visitors' area. 'Kábíyèsí o, *oba gbo gbo, aláyélúwà* (King of all, the omniscient),' greeted Ifálóyé as he rose to his feet. He bowed his head to the King. 'Mo júbà o.'

Adéorí walked towards his throne and settled into his golden chair before waving his staff at Ifálóyé, signalling for him to sit. 'Thank you, Ifálóyé, for your prompt response to my call. May you live long, and may your expertise continue to be relevant to the palace and our great kingdom.'

'*Àse oba* (Amen, my King),' Ifálóyé responded, paying careful attention to the King.

'I have asked one of my personal guards to fetch Queen Adéníké. I am sure she will be here any moment. She has not been feeling well for a few days, although when I visited her earlier today, she looked better. I suspect she could be pregnant, and I would like you to examine her.'

'As your lordship pleases.'

Following this, Queen Adéníké walked into the visitors' area with Àlàbí right behind her. Adéníké looked brighter than she'd looked when the King had seen her earlier, and that made the King glad to see his beautiful queen as she walked toward him. She knelt to greet him as usual, and he pulled her up before her knees touched the ground, asking her to sit on the chair beside the throne meant for the queens. Once the Queen settled into her seat, she extended greetings to Ifálóyé, who had stood up to acknowledge her presence when she'd walked in. The King then waved his staff towards Àlàbí, and the guard proceeded out of the room, leaving King Adéorí, the Queen, and Ifálóyé alone.

Speaking to Adénìké, Adéorí said, 'My beautiful Queen, I have invited the medicine man here as promised to conduct a proper examination on you to make sure your state of health is optimal. I wasn't satisfied when I saw you earlier today, and as you know by now, your well-being is most important to me.'

'Awww... my husband and my lord,' Adénìké exclaimed, looking very pleased, 'that is so thoughtful of you. Yes, you mentioned earlier that you thought I required further examination, but I didn't realize it would be so soon. Interestingly, I have been feeling better since you came to see me this morning, but Ifáló̩yé's examination will be helpful as well. One can never be too healthy,' she said with her usual pretty smile.

'I am pleased to be at your service, your majesty and my Queen,' said Ifáló̩yé.

'Great. Shall we?' the King said as he got up from his throne.

Ifáló̩yé rose also, and Queen Adénìké followed suit. The King led the way into another room directly connected to the visitors' area. In this room were three small beds and very large windows. Beautiful multi-coloured, *àdìre* (tied and dyed) cloth served as curtains that could be drawn to cover the open windows, providing excellent ventilation. Ifáló̩yé was familiar with the room, having previously visited a few times to perform examinations at the King's request.

He walked to the nearest window and pulled the àdìre curtain to cover most of the opening.

Queen Adénìké lay down on her back on the first bed at the request of the medicine man. Shortly thereafter, Ifáló̩yé began examining the Queen, looking at her eyes, tongue, mouth, and throat while the King looked patiently on.

After a continuous examination of the Queen in complete silence for about ten minutes, Ifáló̩yé finally spoke. He smiled at the Queen and politely told her that he was done, indicating that she could sit up. She rose to a sitting position, and Ifáló̩yé began to speak.

'Kábíyèsí o. Thank you for giving me the opportunity to serve you again,' said Ifáló̩yé. 'From all indications, olorì is doing fine. She seems to have had an *ibà* (fever), but I can see her eyes are brighter. Her mouth is still somewhat dry. I will prepare some herbs as soon as I return home and send my son, Ifákúnlé, to bring them later this evening. The herbs will help her body's system heal. I recommend she eats plenty of fruit, too, but other than that, she is fine, Your Majesty,' he said with a convincing smile, looking first at the King and then at the Queen.

King Adéorí finally felt some relief after all the negative thoughts that had been ravaging his mind. 'I secretly wished olorì was carrying our baby,' he said with a chuckle.

'That would be wonderful, your Majesty,' said Ifáló̩yé, 'but no, I am certain olorì is not pregnant.'

'I wish I *was* pregnant, my husband,' commented Queen Adénìké. 'Today would have been the happiest day of my life.'

Ifáló̩yé replied, '*Oló̩dùmarè ní fun ni ló̩mo* (It is the almighty that gives a child). He will give you one and bless the palace in due time.'

'*Àse* (Amen),' the King and Queen said simultaneously. The examination was done, and Ifáló̩yé picked up his leopard skin bag.

Adénìké got up from the bed, and they all walked back into the visitors' area. Queen Adénìké felt an unexplainable but fulfilling relief. As soon as the King and Ifáló̩yé made themselves comfortable in the visitors' area, she asked to leave for her chambers so she could get some more rest. She hugged the King, thanked Ifálóyé, and left, feeling like a new person. Adéníké knew she had escaped this abomination by the skin of her teeth. Her abominable decision to get rid of the result of her unfaithfulness without delay was her only way out of the situation.

'*Elèdá mi mo dúpé o* (Thank you, my creator),' she murmured after she stepped out of the King's chambers and proceeded to hers. On the day Ìyá alágbo had visited her—barely nine days ago—and confirmed that she was pregnant, Adéníké convinced her to prepare a concoction that would remove the unwanted baby. Ìyá alágbo understood the magnitude of the potential trouble the Queen would face if news of such an abomination leaked into the palace and the public. She agreed to help and also to keep her secret. She promised the Queen that her secret was safe and no person born of a woman would hear it from her even upon her last breath. The practice of terminating a pregnancy was very uncommon and seen as an act of taboo that could bring the wrath of the gods upon the culprit, but for Adéníké, a queen becoming pregnant by a palace servant was a greater taboo. This was the one time it felt right for her to tackle one bad deed with another.

The thoughts kept coming as she continued on her way to her chambers, and she found it more and more difficult to hold back the tears from rolling down her cheeks. In the midst of feeling sorry for herself, she was also happy she'd acted fast and used the concoction Ìyá alágbo had sent to her. If not, how would she have handled Ifálóyé's unplanned examination? The fear and worry had literally consumed her and taken over her thoughts beforehand.

As she drew closer to her chambers, she remembered Oláolú—the palace servant in question—for the first time that day. '*Oláolú fé kó bá mi* (Oláolú wants to put me in trouble),' she said quietly. *God forbid...this will never happen again*, she thought, as she walked through her garden towards the entrance with a lighter heart than that with which she had left.

In the evening of the same day, while Queen Olúfúnké was preparing the King's dinner, one of the palace guards brought her news of the presence of her father, the Basòrun, in the King's chambers and that he would like to see her. As Basòrun of Ìkirè Kingdom and the King's childhood friend, Chief Oláòsebìkan was one of the very few people who had access to the King and the palace at almost any time.

Knowing full well the importance of understanding the desired mode of operations and method of doing business prior to negotiations, King Adéorí had tasked the Basòrun with reporting detailed findings of the British businessmen and their company in preparation for the meeting at the Oòni of Ifè's palace in a fortnight. His intention was to empower himself and the other kings who would be present with information enabling them to make optimal business decisions since the meeting had the potential to lead to long-term trade agreements with the new prospective partners.

The Basòrun had brought some news for the King. More often than not, he used such visits to the palace to see his only daughter, and that day was no different. Queen Olúfúnké was almost done making the dinner she would take to the King's chambers. She usually ate dinner with him alone, but as soon as she learned of her father's presence, she decided to prepare additional food so her father could join them. She also planned to invite the older queens to join them as well.

Of course, bàá mi *(my father) wouldn't mind*, she thought as she put more *èko* (cornmeal) and *moí moí* (steamed bean pudding) into the calabash gourd. Olúfúnké intended to break the news of her pregnancy to the King at dinner. Now, she had the opportunity to kill two birds with one stone by telling both the King and her father at the same time. The idea sounded lovely to her since they were the two most important men in her life. Olúfúnké finished packing more than enough food and instructed her maidens to take it to the King's chambers while she went to take a bath and dress in something nice before joining them.

FOUR

———◦•◦———

It is of the utmost importance that we have a balanced deal, your highness,' the Basórun continued. 'Based on your request, my lord, I found out that this group of British businessmen have business ties with the people of the *Arewa* (Northern region). They appear to be credible men though some of my sources from the area have complained that agreements were not properly made, and business dealings have been unbalanced in tremendous favour of the British businessmen. My research also led me to more findings about the types of crops they've shown interest in, in addition to those they plan to discuss at the coming meeting. Here is a list of the crops, your Majesty.' Chief Oláòsebìkan paused as he reached into his leopard-skin pouch for the list he had made and handed it over to the King.

'Thank you, Basòrun,' replied King Adéorí. 'You have done well. I am sure the Oòni and the other kings have also gathered their own findings. I believe that with our joint efforts, we will negotiate appropriately to ensure the benefit of our region and people.'

The Basòrun agreed. 'Yes, Your Highness. This research is very important since our preferred options are long-term agreements, and any shortcomings in such agreements will affect us all. I am awaiting additional information from my sources, and we will have more details before your scheduled meeting, my King.' The Basòrun was the King's favoured person for discussions on matters pertaining to trade. His knowledge encompassed the Yoruba land and beyond. The Basòrun's skill was mainly attributed to heredity because both his father and grandfather were great traders who had played similar roles in Ìkirè Kingdom to the King's ancestors.

As the two men continued their conversation about the upcoming meeting, they heard a knock on the door of the private meeting room in which they were holding their discussion. King Adéorí only conducted meetings in the room with close cabinet members. Since the King wasn't expecting anyone, both men wondered who could be knocking.

'Come in,' the King said in a deep, commanding tone.

The door opened, and Olúfúnké walked into the room.

Her father smiled as soon as he saw her.

'*Aya oba* (Wife of a king),' said the King.

Olúfúnké walked toward her husband to greet him. She knelt before him and placed her hands on his knees while he hugged her and patted her back.

'Get up, my dear. What a pleasant surprise. Did you know your father was here?' he asked.

'Yes, my King,' replied the Queen. 'I knew bàá mi was here with you.' She got up from her position and went to where her father sat to greet him as well. *'Ekú alé, bàá mi* (Good evening, my father).'

'Good evening, my darling daughter. Or better yet, good evening, my Queen,' Chief Oláòsebìkan said with a proud smile.

'I am still your daughter, bàá mi,' Olúfúnké responded with a girlish smile. 'How are màá mi and my brothers?' she asked.

'They are all doing fine, and they send their greetings,' he answered. 'Especially your mother. She asked me to tell you that she misses you so much and is looking forward to when you will visit her.'

'I miss her, too, and intend to visit soon, bàá mi. I miss everyone, although my husband is making sure I do not miss you all too much.'

King Adéorí nodded with a chuckle at Olúfúnké's last statement. 'I know you have come here to inform me that dinner is ready, and you had to interrupt our meeting because you don't want the food to get cold,' he said.

Olúfúnké rolled her eyes at her husband in a loving manner before responding, 'Yes, my King. You know me too well. You and bàá mi can have dinner now and continue with your discussion after eating. I am also hungry, so for my sake, it would be better if we eat now.' The two men laughed at Olúfúnké's comment.

'Okay, my lovely Queen,' Adéorí said. 'Basòrun, I think Olúfúnké has a great idea. Please, join us for dinner, and we shall continue our conversation after eating.'

'Thank you, Your Majesty. Dinner will be ready in five minutes,' she said before rushing out of the room. King Adéorí and the Basòrun wrapped up their talk and left for dinner.

Olúfúnké had informed the older queens on her way to the King's chambers, as she often had before. She made sure to stop at the older queens' chambers herself because of her plan to share news of her pregnancy with all of them at the same time. Her father's presence was an unexpected yet welcome surprise.

King Adéorí, his three queens, and the Basòrun all sat around the round, beautifully carved table to eat dinner. Olúfúnké, who sat close to her father, served everyone, and once she'd returned to her seat, the King started with a prayer as he usually did: 'May the gods of our land and my ancestors bless and purify this food. May we eat the food in peace, digest the food in peace, and continue to live to eat another meal in peace.'

'Àse,' said the queens and the Basòrun, and they all began eating the amazing delicacies Olúfúnké had prepared. The maidens brought in some palm wine, and the group continued in blissful silence. The only sound in the room was chewing as the wine was served round.

Queen Adéòsun took a big sip of the palm wine that had been poured for her by the maiden. 'Olúfúnké, our wife,' she began. She often referred to Olúfúnké as 'our wife' to acknowledge her as the youngest wife in the palace. 'This is some of the best moi moi I have had in a very long time. The wine compliments it well, and everything tastes so good. Dinner couldn't have been better tonight,' she added as she stretched forward to pick up another wrap of moi moi from the clay calabash placed at the centre of the table.

Moi moi and èko were popular food combinations in Ìkirè and often prepared for dinner because they were light. Èko and moi moi were wrapped in leaves and cooked until well done, then served immediately. Queen Olúfúnké had added some dried fish—also known as black fish—and eggs to her moi moi, making it an absolute delight on the tongue.

King Adéorí nodded his head in affirmation of the older queen's comment. Undoubtedly, the meal tasted very good.

'*Omo tí a kó tó gbèkó* (A child whom we taught and who also allowed herself to be taught),' stated the Basòrun. 'She learnt well from her mother after many years of getting it wrong. Only her mother can tell us how much work she had to do before she heeded the cooking lessons received. I'm sure her mother would be proud, and as for me, I feel as if I am eating her mother's food.'

Olúfúnké smiled and felt very happy to hear the wonderful comments about her cooking, yet all she could think of was her special news. She waited patiently for the right time to share the joyous announcement.

Queen Adéníké, who was also enjoying her meal, didn't make any comments, but she also shared a smile at the Basòrun's comments about his daughter.

The group finished eating dinner, and the maidens came in to clear the table. As the first maiden cleared the last bit from the table and the second maiden served them another round of wine, Olúfúnké began feeling nervous about her plan, and she tried to calm herself.

Once the second maiden had left the room, Olúfúnké stood up to speak: 'Kábíyèsí o, my lord and my husband,' the Queen began. 'I greet you again with warmth, my King. I want to use this opportunity to thank you for all you have done for me since I came into the palace as your wife. Your wisdom, guidance, and protection are unquantifiable.' She paused for a brief moment.

King Adéorí wasn't sure why Olúfúnké was thanking him, but of course, he was used to receiving loving words of praise and adoration from his queens.

Upon seeing the King's broad smile and obvious admiration, Olúfúnké carried on: 'I also want to thank you, bàá mi. You have been the strongest pillar of support I have ever known, and it makes me so happy that you are here today to eat with my family and share this wonderful moment with us.' She looked at her father with a childlike smile, turned to the older queens, and continued: 'And to *Ìyálé mi* (my older wives), thank you for your support and for accepting me as a member and part of the family. May you all live long enough to reap the fruits of your labour and continue to support the hope and liberation of our great land.'

'Àse,' they all responded, Queen Adéòsun's voice resonating the loudest. Adéòsun had her suspicions about where the conversation was going since Olúfúnké had told her the news earlier. Everyone else was curious as to what Olúfúnké's speech was about, and another moment of silence befell the room.

'I have good news for you, my precious family: I am pregnant,' announced Queen Olúfúnké. 'The medicine man also confirmed it a few days ago, but I told him not to mention it to anyone until I shared the news myself.' She looked at the King and saw his expression of surprise.

While he was still processing the information, Queen Adéòsun jumped up from her seat with excitement and began dancing and singing. '*Ayò mí tidé o, ayò mí tidé* (My joy has arrived, my happiness has arrived). *Láti èní lo títí laílaí ayò mí tidé o* (From today onwards and forever more, my joy has arrived)!'

As the older queen sang away, King Adéorí rose from his seat and walked towards Olúfúnké. He hugged her and then looked deep into her eyes before whispering quietly, 'Are you sure about this, my Queen? You are carrying my child? My creation? An heir to Ìkirè Kingdom?'

'Yes, my husband. I am so excited!' replied Olúfúnké. 'I wasn't sure how to tell you, but yes, yes, yes, I am.'

King Adéorí could not contain his excitement, nor could he express how he felt. He raised his hands to the sky and thanked Olódùmarè for his kindness and for gracing him by allowing him to see this day.

The Basòrun, who was probably the happiest amongst them all, also got up to hug his daughter. His reaction was very calm as he had expected this to happen. This news was a major milestone achieved towards the execution of his plan. '*Okáre omo mí, omo olá, àjí rí dunnú* (Well done, my child. A child born in wealth, one who brings you joy when you set your eyes on her in the morning after waking up),' he told her. 'You have made me proud today, and I am sure your mother will be very happy to hear this news.'

'Thank you, bàá mi,' Queen Olúfúnké replied. 'None of this would have been possible without you. If I came into this world again, bàá mi, I would choose you as my father,' she said as tears rolled down her cheeks.

Queen Adénìké had been watching everyone closely, and she wasn't sure how to react to the news. The mood in the room was electrifying and contagious at the same time. Although she had gone through a lot in the last few days, she also felt great happiness for Olúfúnké. Adénìké realized *she* could have been the one sharing news of her own pregnancy if she had obeyed and not left to see her friends when the King had married the younger queen. So many different thoughts ran through her mind concurrently, but she composed herself quickly and reminded herself it wasn't the right time to worry about her own problems. The least she could do now was to be happy for the young queen who had come into the palace to give their kingdom hope for the future. Adénìké shrugged off her worries and stepped out of the room to summon one of the maidens to bring in some more wine for a toast.

The King and Basòrun were seated at the table again while Queen Adéòsun stood speaking quietly with Olúfúnké. Adénìké returned to the room, and the other two queens sat down at the table. A maiden walked in with a jar of wine and filled their cups while Adénìké took her seat at the table. Once the maiden was done, she took her leave, and Queen Adénìké stood up to make a toast.

'Kábíyèsí o,' she said as she bowed her head before her husband. 'With the permission of Your Majesty, the Basòrun of our great land, *ìyálé mi* (the wife before me),' Adénìké said, looking at Queen Adéòsun, 'and *ìyàwó mi* (the wife after me),' she said, looking at Queen Olúfúnké, 'today marks a great occasion and wonderful day in our lives and most especially for the palace and our great kingdom. Words cannot express my feelings since Olúfúnké shared her news with us, and based on this glorious day, I request your permission to say a toast.' She raised up her cup of wine and waited until everyone else in the room had done the same before continuing.

'To the progress of Ìkirè and our beloved King. To the queens, our unborn children, and our future generations. And most especially, to the baby who isn't here with us yet, but who, I am sure, can hear us today.' They all laughed. She ended the toast by pledging, 'Kábíyèsí o.'

They all stood up to clink their cups with calls of *'Ayò ni ò, kára ó le* (Cheers, good health)!' all around. The atmosphere for the rest of the evening was filled with jokes and laughter, and they all chatted away until the King and the Basòrun left to finish up their meeting, and the queens returned to their chambers to conclude the celebration.

After another two hours of discussion with the Basòrun in the private room, King Adéorí retired to his chambers. It was now one hour before midnight, and the evening had been very eventful, considering Olúfúnké's news as well as the manner in which she'd made the announcement. The day, as a whole, had been exceptional, beginning with uncertainties and ending with some level of certainty. The King removed his *fìlà* (cap) and agbádá before sitting down on the wooden rocking chair next to his bed. He wondered whether everything that had happened from the time he'd awoken until now was not all connected. He contemplated it all for a few moments and tried to find a connection but decided the effort was futile.

He awakened his thoughts again to the news of an heir—his own flesh and blood, soon to be borne by Olúfúnké into the palace. He smiled and spoke out loud: 'I think the connection I am looking for is the one I have found tonight. My child will be born a few months from now, and my energy will become double and renewed.' He dropped to his knees and said a prayer to the gods of the land and his ancestors, especially thanking them for gracing him with seeing that day.

As soon as King Adéorí sat back in his bedside chair, he heard a knock on the door. He wasn't expecting anyone, nor had he called for anyone to come to his chambers. It could only be one of his queens or personal guards.

'Come in, whoever you may be,' King Adéorí invited, his sonorous voice resounding across the entire room.

The door opened, and to the King's surprise, his beautiful Queen Adénìké walked in. Her figure was well-defined as the rays of light from the lanterns in the corners of the King's room shone on her and through her purple dress. Her beautiful hair was smoothed back, and her royal golden necklace and beads glowed around her neck and wrists as she approached her husband. Adénìké was the epitome of beauty, and the sight of her was enough to make any man short on words. The door closed behind her, and the King watched as she walked elegantly towards him without saying a word.

She knelt down in front of her husband, held his hands, and kissed him on the cheek before saying, '*Olówó orí mi, okoò mi, olólùfé mi, eni okàn mí yán* (The one who paid my dowry, my husband, my lover, the one my heart chooses and desires).' The Queen kissed him again, this time on his lips, whilst looking seductively into his eyes.

Adéorí was pleasantly surprised at Adénìké's gesture, and he didn't know what to say. He remained mute as he watched her, knowing that she was very open with showing affection. She kissed his lips again, this time for a little longer, and the King slowly began to understand why she was there.

'My sweet, beautiful Dénìké,' said the King, 'I wasn't expecting to see you. But—'

Adénìké interrupted. 'Yes, my love. Are you not glad that I am here now?' she asked with a smile as she rubbed her fingers across his chest and down to his belly.

'Oh, of course I am,' Adéorí replied. 'You know I am always glad to see you, and I adore you, but you did not mention at dinner that you would be coming to see me to discuss anything with me tonight.'

'Yes, my love. I hadn't planned to come here tonight. I was only thinking to myself barely half an hour ago about Olúfúnké's good news, and that inspired me. We have always wanted to have a child in this palace, and I think we will have more than one, my lord. We will have *children* in this palace. The reason I am here tonight is to receive mine, Your Majesty.'

'To receive yours? What do you mean, Dénìké?' asked the King.

'I have come to receive my own child, *okoò mí* (my husband).' She kissed him again on the lips before he could respond and proceeded to kiss him slowly all over. She stood and pulled down her dress to reveal her bare skin and amazing curves.

At that point, the King was all in. He pulled his beautiful Dénìké closer to him. She sat on his lap, and they began kissing deeply as his hands wandered around her body, touching her in all of the tender places. Adénìké moaned with pleasure when she felt the King's hands between her legs. It couldn't have felt better. She realized how much she had missed him, and it was obvious he had missed her too. She got up from his lap and went down on her husband, licking and kissing every inch of him as she had never done before. The night had only just begun as the two lovebirds explored each other and made steamy love before eventually falling asleep in one another's arms.

FIVE

———◦|◦———

The news of Olúfúnké's pregnancy spread throughout the palace within a few days. The saying, 'The walls have ears,' was true of the palace. Activities in the palace continued as usual, but from all indications, the news was well received, and the presence of this new, unborn life brought about hopefulness in the palace, even though the King had not yet officially proclaimed the news to the kingdom. Those who had been patiently waiting for the day an heir would be born into the palace of their beloved King had begun to count the days to the child's delivery. It could be said that the entire kingdom of Ìkirè was expecting a child.

Olúfúnké's mother, Rómoké, received the news the same night her daughter had told her father, and she was extremely happy. The thought of her daughter's child—her grandchild and heir to the great kingdom—caused her nothing short of excitement and great joy. Knowing that she would be visiting her daughter more often, she started making plans to help and support her daughter on her journey to motherhood.

The sun had just begun to set in the evening of the same day when the servants returned to the palace from working on the farm. As usual, Oláolú led the servants to the farm. His job of leading and controlling the servants to achieve optimum results on the farm was very tasking and not a lazy man's job. The guards who had accompanied the servants also did a tremendous job of keeping the whole process steady. More often than not, others wondered whether anyone else could coordinate the activities as well as Oláolú, as he was a naturally talented leader who performed his tasks effortlessly. The majority of the servants under his control liked him, aside from the few who felt oppressed or intimidated by the way he managed and ordered them around.

That day had been extraordinary, as they had more work to do than usual on the farm. The two thirty-minute breaks they were usually allowed on a workday were cut in half, and the servants were all very tired as the guards led them back to the palace. The servants were an interesting sight to see as they moved from the farm through the village and back to the palace in large groups.

Oláolú walked slowly with his friends, Àlàní and Gbadé. The group they were a part of was separated from the last guard by only a few yards. A group of servants was walking somewhat closely behind them, and various other groups of servants, both small and large, were walking together and chatting away. As expected, Àlàní was doing most of the talking as the three men carried on their conversation in the midst of the larger group returning to the palace.

'I am so hungry, my friends. *Mo lè je ilé pèlú irú ebi tó ńpa mí yì* (I could eat a house with the type of hunger I feel right now),' Àlàní said, frowning.

'Àlàní, you are just too funny,' replied Gbadé. 'Everyone, including you, knows that you could eat a whole house at any time. Are you always this hungry, or should we expect to see a phenomenal level of consumption from you today?'

Oláolú, along with some servants who walked in close proximity, heard Gbadé's response and laughed. Àlàní shook his head as though he was contemplating reacting to Gbadé, but before he could utter a word, his friend continued.

'Anyway, you wouldn't need to search too far off to find enough to eat. I think you should consider eating the whole of Queen Adéníké's chambers. You know, there are some trees behind her chamber building. You could consume them with the building, and if that's not enough, you could eat the maidens, too. You won't be able to eat the Queen, though, or Your Highness will kill you. I know you wouldn't mind if you were allowed to, Mister I-can-eat-a-house,' teased Gbadé.

'Shut your mouth, Gbadé,' Àlàní retorted. 'Aren't you tired? You're making me even hungrier. When I said that, it did not mean that I wanted to *literally* eat a whole house, you dumb servant.'

Gbadé laughed out loud because he knew he had gotten under Àlàní's thick skin, which was a rare occurrence. 'Don't be mad, my friend,' he said. 'I was just joking with you, but what's the difference between someone who eats *as much as* a house and someone who eats a house?' he asked, continuing to pull Àlàní's leg.

'Gbadé, I think Àlàní is really hungry today,' Oláolú added. 'Please, have some mercy on him. You remember the saying, "A hungry man is an angry man," right?'

'That's very true. You are absolutely correct. I should not be joking with a hungry Àlàní,' said Gbadé.

'That's your business. I will have time for you once I have had something to eat. Enjoy this moment while it lasts,' Àlàní said quietly as though he were trying not to exhaust anymore of his energy by talking.

'It is interesting to know that days like this exist, Àlàní; a day when you would prefer to stay quiet rather than talk, *oba àwon sòrò sòrò* (king of the talkative),' Oláolú said with a smile.

'On second thought, Àlàní,' said Gbadé, 'when I suggested you could eat the maidens, I was remembering one of Queen Adénìké's maidens, Omolará. Come to think of it, I can't believe I said that.' He smiled, amused. 'One of the two maidens who went with us the last time the Queen visited her friends in Ede. You were crushing on her and have been following her around with the hope of wooing her ever since we got back from the trip. *Bí omo adìe tó ń tèlé ìya rè kiri* (Like a chick following the mother hen everywhere). What is the situation with her, my friend?'

With a look of disgust, Àlàní responded, 'You are the one who will come back to this world as a chicken when you die. *Ahón re mú ní ìròlé yì* (Your tongue is sharp this evening). You're lucky I'm so hungry and need more strength to talk. If not, what I would have said to you today, *etí re kòní lè gbá* (your ears wouldn't have been able to hear without getting hurt). Anyway, Oláolú is the one with the answer to your question, so you should channel it to him. He is in the best position to tell us more about Omolará and her whereabouts. *Bámi bí o. Óti gbà lówó mi* (Ask him for me. He has taken her from me),' he said, glaring at Oláolú.

'Ha, Àlàní,' said Gbadé, 'that is a huge allegation against Oláolú.'

'Well, why don't you ask him? Isn't he right here? After all, I said what I said in his presence.'

Oláolú had been listening to the conversation all the while but ignored them and acted as though he could not hear what his friends were saying. He was definitely guilty of Àlàní's allegations. His eyes met with Gbadé's, and he suddenly looked away, hoping he would drop the topic and move onto something else. But Gbadé, being the fearless and interrogative type, continued to press on with the subject. He could tell that Àlàní was speaking the truth because Oláolú was popularly known amongst the servants in the kingdom as having the ability to cajole maidens easily with his looks and status in the palace. Whether that was his fault or the maidens' was another topic for discussion.

Gbadé addressed Oláolú directly: 'Why don't you respond to Àlàní's claims, Oláolú? The *alágbára (the powerful one)* amongst servants of our dear kingdom—I know you very well. Your lack of a response indicates to me that you are guilty as charged. Without your response, I am inclined to believe Àlàní's claims because I have encountered something similar with you before. Anyway, not to worry, Àlàní, my friend, God will bring your own woman to you soon.'

An awkward silence settled amongst the three men as they continued back to the palace, although the other servants in the group continued chatting and laughing away. They arrived at the entrance to the palace around half-past six. The servants residing inside the palace went in while the larger majority proceeded to the houses that had been built for the servants on a sizable expanse of land behind the palace.

For most of their remaining journey back to the palace, Oláolú hadn't stopped thinking about the complaints his friends had made about him. The three men entered the palace premises before Oláolú decided to speak. '*Mábìnú sí mi òré mi, Àlàní* (Don't be upset with me, my friend, Àlàní). There is no other way to view the incident with Omolará. She pushed herself on me, but that is not an excuse. As a man, I should have been able to take a stand, especially knowing that my friend liked her. Don't be mad at me,' he said with a morose and guilty look on his face.

Gbadé smiled, and Àlàní nodded his head at Oláolú without saying a word. The three men walked to their various rooms to freshen up after the long day of farm work, after which they settled in to have dinner.

On the morning of Thursday, December 15, eight days after the minor altercation between Àlàní and Oláolú over Omolará, Queen Adénìké's maiden, some of the servants who had completed their morning chores were having breakfast while the others were just wrapping up. Oláolú sat to have breakfast in the palace canteen with his friends, Àlàní, Gbadé, and Túnjí. Breakfast included *dùndún* (fried sweet cocoyam) and *epo pupa* (palm oil). The dùndún, a renowned Yorùbá delicacy, tasted so good, and they greatly enjoyed their breakfast.

The servants received one day off work weekly, usually every Thursday, to take care of personal things and receive friends and family visitors. Servants were also permitted to have palm wine on their day off and serve it to their guests. The atmosphere in the palace canteen was alive and noisy because the wine supply had begun to flow. Most of those in the canteen laughed out loud and spoke in high tones as they ate breakfast and drank wine. Oláolú and his friends finished breakfast but remained in the canteen, clutching their cups of wine and chatting away. As expected, Àlàní—the jester—was dishing out jokes and making his friends laugh when one of the palace guards came into the canteen to make an announcement.

The announcement was to call Oláolú's attention as he had a visitor waiting for him in the palace's visiting hall. It was quite early to begin having visitors, but when Oláolú heard his name, he got up from where he was sitting with his friends, stepped out of the canteen, and headed to the visiting hall with the palace guard.

Oláolú and the guard arrived at the visiting hall and walked in through the rear door to find his younger sister, Omósaléwá, sitting on one of the wooden chairs designated for visitors. She wore a blue *àdìre ìró àti bùbá* (tied and dyed wrapper and blouse) decorated with leaf designs. Her hair was plaited, and her features were very attractive. She displayed a striking resemblance to her brother, such that an onlooker could tell from a distance that they were fruits bore of the same tree. Although Oláolú remembered he had sent a message home to his mother earlier in the week, asking her to send Omósaléwá over that day to run an important errand, he still wondered if the visitor was someone else as he walked down to the hall with the guard. As soon as he saw his sister, he became calmer and felt some relief as he walked over to her.

Oláolú tapped Omósaléwá on the shoulder, and she turned to see who it was. 'Saléwá,' he said, lightly squeezing her shoulder.

At the sound of her brother's voice, she turned her head and jumped from her seat to hug him. She had missed seeing him so much. Omósaléwá viewed her brother as a guardian, big brother, and father figure since they'd lost their father fifteen years ago. They hugged for a minute before sitting down together, side by side, to talk.

'*Saléwá, àbúrò mi tòótó—báwo ni gbogbo ǹkan* (Saléwá, my sincere younger sister–how is everything)?' he asked.

'*Dáada ni mo wà* (I am doing very well),' she answered.

'*Màámi ǹkó* (How about my mother)? *Shé àlááfià ni àwon náà wà* (I hope she is also doing well)?'

'Yes, she is fine, brother. She sends greetings and asked me to tell you that she misses you so much and looks forward to when you will visit home next.'

'*Láì pé* (Very soon),' said Oláolú. 'I miss her so much, and you, too. You must have left home very early. I am glad màá mi received my message asking you to arrive early today. You won't believe that I'd totally forgotten I was expecting you until the guard came to fetch me.'

'Ha, *ègbón mi* (my older brother). I am glad that I met you, then. It would have been painful if I'd arrived and was told that you were not around.' Oláolú's mother and sister lived in a small village about an hour's walk away from the palace.

'I would have been sad if you hadn't also since I asked you to come here for a particular reason. Today is a free day for me, and the likelihood that I would be out of the palace today is very slim. Do you want me to get you anything to drink or eat?'

'No, brother. I am doing okay,' replied Omósaléwá. 'If I need something, I will let you know. Màá mi said I should give these food items to you.' She pointed at a bag on the floor beside her. 'Màá mi says it should last you for some time before she sends you more.'

'That's so sweet of her. I love you two so much. Thank you, my dear sister,' he said as he took the bag from his sister and stood up. 'I am very happy to see you, my dear sister. Please, I would like you to wait here for me for ten to fifteen minutes. There is something I want you to take back to màá mi for safekeeping. Are you sure you don't want me to get you something to drink at least? It is provided by the palace,' he said with a persuasive smile.

'I am fine, brother Oláolú. If I need something, you know I will tell you even before you have the chance to ask me.'

'Okay, dear. I will be right back.' He picked up the bag of food and walked out of the visiting hall through the same rear door he'd entered, stepping outside into the main palace courtyard.

Oláolú went straight to his room in the servants' quarters to drop off the foodstuff, after which he proceeded to Queen Adéòsun's chambers. Most of the servants were still out enjoying themselves at the canteen, and the quarters were quite empty. Upon arriving at Queen Adéòsun's chambers, he met two maidens who were cleaning the frontage of the building and watering the plants in the queen's garden. Her chambers were known for accommodating more activities because the older queen required more maidens than the other queens, and one project or another was regularly ongoing. The chambers appeared quieter than usual to him that morning; however, as he moved closer to the front entrance where the maidens were working, he heard female voices coming from the rear courtyard behind the chambers.

'*Ekú árò o* (Good morning). *Ekú isé o* (Work well done),' Oláolú said, greeting the maidens as he stood before the main entrance area.

The maidens briefly stopped what they were doing and turned to see who was sending them greetings. They recognized Oláolú, and they both answered, 'Good morning, Oláolú. Thank you.'

'How are you?' asked one of the maidens. 'It is a surprise to see you here this morning. I hope there is no problem.'

'I am doing very well. I came to see the Queen. She asked me to see her this morning. Is she in?'

'Yes, the Queen is in,' she replied. 'Please wait while I inform her that you are here.'

'Thank you very much,' Oláolú said, nodding.

The maiden went into the Queen's chambers while Oláolú gazed around the beautiful garden waiting for her to bring back some news. The other maiden continued watering the plants, singing away in a low tone. Barely two minutes later, the first maiden reappeared and asked Oláolú to come in.

He had been to Queen Adéòsun's chambers a few times in the past, but the beautiful design of the interior always impressed him each time he visited. They walked down a well-lit hallway into a beautifully decorated visitors' room, with which Oláolú was familiar since he had been asked to wait there for the Queen in the past. But that day was different as the maiden walked him past the visitors' waiting area into a larger living area fully decorated with ornaments, sculptures, and paintings.

'Her Majesty, the Queen, asked me to bring you here. Please, take a seat, and she will be with you shortly,' said the maiden.

'Thank you.' His mind wandered as he looked around the gorgeous living area. He sat down on a small stool. It was the first time he had been allowed into the living area. He had always considered the visitors room where he waited for the Queen very beautiful, but this place was twice as magnificent in his eyes. He continued to look around in awe, imagining what the King's living area must look like. Not very long afterwards, his thoughts were interrupted by the sound of the Queen's voice. 'Oláolú,' Queen Adéòsun called out as she walked into the living room.

Oláolú stood then and went on his knees to greet the Queen. She was elegantly dressed as always and represented royalty in every form and sense of the word. 'Good morning, Your Majesty, my Queen, the mother of our great kingdom.'

'Good morning, Oláolú. How are you doing today?' asked the Queen.

'I am well, Your Majesty.'

'Wonderful,' she said as she proceeded to sit on the ornate gold chair across the room from Oláolú. '*Dìde ńlè* (Rise from the floor).'

He rose, then seated himself on the stool again.

'I won't take up too much of your time, Oláolú,' said Queen Adéòsun. 'I believe that you have made arrangements for someone to take what I am about to present to you to a safe place as I directed you the last time we spoke.'

'Yes, my Queen. I sent a message home, and my sister is here, waiting in the visiting hall. She will take the item to my mother, and I am sure it will remain safe.'

'That's good. I am pleased that you thought of your family. *A kòle rí inú eni torí inú ènìyàn jìnà* (We cannot see what is inside a person because the inside of a person is very deep). *Tí a bá sì ma finú han eni, kòsí eni tí ó dàbí awo àti èjè eni* (And if we want to open up and show someone what's inside us, no one is like one's own flesh and blood),' she added.

Oláolú nodded his head in acknowledgement of what the Queen had said.

Adéòsun continued. *'Ó yán si mí létí lénu ojó méta pé ó seése kí Adénìké ti férakù* (It has come to my knowledge these past few days that Adénìkè is likely pregnant). And we know what has been going on. Well done. I have seen your work, and you have performed beyond my expectations.'

Oláolú smiled at the Queen's praises, although it was the first time he had heard that Queen Adénìké could be pregnant. The revelation surprised him, but he kept his cool.

'Very soon, this will be confirmed, and the palace will know. *Òrò tí a kò fé kí baba ó gbó, baba ní ó parí rè* (The issue we don't want Father to know about, the same father will help resolve),' she said, buttressing her point with another adage. She picked up a cream-coloured bag resting on the floor beside her. 'Take this bag,' she instructed, holding it out to him.

Oláolú approached the Queen and accepted the bag from her with a bow.

'That bag is full of gold coins enough for two lifetimes. It is all for you. Make sure it is brought to your mother for safekeeping as planned. *Sùgbón ìkìlò kán wà* (But be warned). *Etí méjì míràn kò gbodò báwa gbó ńkan tí a sè o* (Another pair of ears must not hear what we have cooked up). This is very important for everyone's wellbeing, and I am sure I do not have to reiterate this to you again because you understand perfectly well.'

'Yes, my Queen,' Oláolú answered. 'You can rest assured. *Kòsí eni kéni tí a bí láti inú obìrin tí yìò gbó ńkan tí a sè láti enu mí* (No person born from a woman will hear what we have cooked up from me). I am eternally grateful for this gift, my Queen. I never expected such generosity. Thank you very much, Your Majesty, mother of our great kingdom.'

Queen Adéòsun made a dismissive gesture. '*Kò tópé* (It is not worth the thanks). You deserve it. Be sure to see me again in about three weeks. You may take your leave now.'

'I will return as you wish, my Queen. Thank you for everything,Your Majesty. I am very grateful.' Gripping the bag tightly, he bowed his head to the Queen before walking out of the living area and Adéòsun's chambers with his newly-acquired fortune.

Oláolú walked back to the visiting area where his sister would be waiting for him, his thoughts racing in multiple directions. He saw himself as a very strong man, but the presence of the older queen always consumed him in an inexplicable way. Obviously, she was a strong force to be reckoned with and one that exuded much wisdom. He looked at the bag the Queen had given him with a smile of relief. He had not had the chance to examine the contents yet, but he heard gold coins clink together. He already felt his transformation from a poor, ordinary servant begin, and he silently thanked Olódùmarè for bringing such fortune his way. '*Kò sí eni tín bèrè bí ase kó orò jo; orò ni orò ń jé* (Nobody asks how wealth is acquired; wealth is wealth). My family and I will never be poor again,' he whispered to himself as he approached the entrance of the visiting area.

Omósaléwá was still sitting, waiting patiently, and she smiled as soon as she saw him. '*Ègbón mi* (my older brother), you took so long,' she said. 'I was beginning to think you'd forgotten me here and had gone back to doing other things.'

'*Àbúrò* (younger sibling), don't be upset with me. I did not expect to take as long as I did. The delay was for our own good. You know it would not be possible for me to forget that you were here,' he responded, smiling. 'The items and message I want you to take to màá mi are what kept me a little longer.'

Oláolú rubbed his sister's head as though he were caressing a pet before sitting down beside her. The visiting hall was quiet, and the two siblings appeared to be alone. He took a cautious look around to make absolutely sure no one was watching them before placing the bag of gold coins on the table and looking inside for the first time. His eyes grew wide and round as the rising sun as he opened the bag. Oláolú had never seen that many gold coins in his entire life.

His sister noticed the abrupt change in his expression and wondered what her brother might be looking at. 'Ègbón mi, what is in the bag that made you react that way?'

'Ha, Saléwá,' Oláolú said. 'Come and see for yourself.' He pushed the bag a little closer to her, enough for her to peek in.

Omósaléwá almost screamed at what she saw. 'Ègbón mi—when have you seen so much gold? Is it for us? Were you sent on an errand with it?'

'This money is for us, àbúrò,' he replied earnestly, 'and you are going to take it home to màá mi for me. You have to be very careful with it. Tie the bag inside your ìró (wrapper) so that no one will see it. Tell màá mi to keep it in a very safe place, and I will soon send a message to her about what we will do with the money. Just make sure you get the bag home safely. That is the most important duty you have now, okay?' Omósaléwá nodded her head as she listened to him.

Oláolú tied the bag firmly, gave it to her, and watched as she hid the bag in her wrapper. 'You can go now, àbúrò. I will see you soon. Tell màá mi that I love her, and I love you, too. This is the end of poverty in our lives. We will never be poor again.'

'Yes, ègbón mi. I love you, too, and I will deliver the message to màá mi,' she said.

Both siblings stood and walked through the door of the visiting area before parting ways. Omósaléwá departed towards the palace entrance gate while Oláolú went back to the dining area to rejoin his friends.

SIX

A few weeks prior, King Adeori received a special invitation from the Oòni of Ifè and the Aláàfin of Òyó, the monarchs spearheading the business relationship between the British company and the Yorùbá land, to attend a meeting as directed by the crowned ueen of Britain. The Oòni and the Aláàfin were the most prominent rulers in the Yorùbá Kingdom, revered by other rulers throughout the region and beyond. According to the invitation that had been signed by the two monarchs and sent to his palace, a positive outcome from the meeting and the negotiations would have the potential to transform the lives and livelihood of the citizens of the Yorùbá land.

King Adéorí felt honoured to be a part of such an important meeting, especially because the invitation he had received indicated that he was expected to give the opening presentation at the negotiations on behalf of the Yorùbá monarchs. Of course, King Adéorí hadn't been selected for this role because of his status as a royal or his close affiliation with the Oòni. The primary motivation was his track record of phenomenal intelligence and business acumen and an outstanding ability to negotiate balanced deals with both local and foreign businessmen.

About a decade before, he'd been instrumental in a major negotiation with one of the first groups of businessmen who had come into the territory to seek business opportunities. That negotiation brought about the creation of the first senior secondary educational institution in the region and also led to the introduction of the Yorùbá language into the educational curriculum. That particular partnership had yielded tremendous results for the Yorùbá people, and it was no surprise to them that Adéorí was not only a King but an avid negotiator who put the collective progress of the people first in all his dealings. Making the people the focal point of his negotiations helped him emerge with strategic deals that had brought tremendous benefits to the people whose land also provided proceeds for the foreign businessmen. He was known for his popular slogan, *'Ìnílò àwon ará ìlú níse àkókó, kí ti wa tó tèle* (the needs of the people come first before ours can follow).' He never failed to reiterate this slogan, and HE carried it with him into all business negotiations, which made his position and where his loyalty lay very clear to everyone.

Later in the afternoon, on the same day that Oláolú met with Queen Adéòsun, the King's entourage was getting ready to leave for the five-hour journey to the Oòni's palace in Ife. On business trips, King Adéorí often travelled alone with his entourage without the company of his queens. His entourage consisted of two chariots with six horses, four personal guards who carried his staff of office and other items, and six fully armed palace guards who took turns controlling the chariot and six servants.

On this occasion, the invitation had suggested the King bring his queens with him because of a ceremony that had been planned to commemorate the meeting. For that reason, four maidens were included in the King's entourage for the queen attending with him.

A few days earlier, King Adéorí had confirmed that his second queen, Adénìké, would be travelling along with him. This decision hadn't come as a surprise to the younger queen, Olúfúnké, but the older queen, Adéòsun, hadn't expected it, and she was upset. Adéòsun had been making plans for the event, assuming the King would bring her as she was the first queen. Even more so because he would be meeting with other top monarchs, and she usually graced such important occasions at his side. She complained and expressed her discontent to the King in the hope he would see some reason and change his mind, but unfortunately, King Adéorí had already made up his mind about which queen would accompany him, and nothing would change it.

While the guards were getting the chariot ready near the King's chambers, Queen Adénìké and her maidens hastily gathered all of the queen's travel items in her chambers. As expected, Adénìké, the queen of beauty, was taking along enough clothing items and belongings to last a full week even though they would return home in two days. Once the guards were done preparing the chariot, they would collect the Queen and her maidens before returning for the King, after which the journey would begin; traditional practice stipulated that for any trip outside the kingdom, the King may only leave directly from his chambers.

Typically, the Queen took much longer to get ready, but on that day, she was ready and waiting in the garden at the entrance of her chambers when the maidens brought out the luggage they would be taking on the trip. Knowing full well that her husband was very time-conscious, the last thing she wanted was to keep him waiting, which would be a sure way to start the journey on a sour note.

As she watched the maidens bring out the luggage, she wondered why the King had chosen her to embark on such an important journey ahead of the older queen. She understood why he had not chosen Olúfúnké, but why not Queen Adéòsun? Everyone who heard about the meeting knew of its importance to the Yorùbá land and that it was also an opportunity for the queens of the various kingdoms to meet, mingle, and engage. What was the King trying to do? What message was he trying to convey by asking her to go with him? Adénìké was full of questions without any answers, but soon enough, she heard the horses neighing and the voices of the King's guards from outside her garden, indicating the chariot had arrived.

The guards came into the Queen's chambers and loaded the luggage onto the chariot. As soon as they were finished, one of the guards helped the Queen into the cabin of the main chariot while the maidens stepped into the cabin of the second chariot. As soon as everyone was settled, they headed straight for the King's chambers. King Adéorí joined Queen Adénìké, and they all set out for Ifè.

The King's entourage arrived at the palace of the Oòni of Ifè late that evening. The journey had been very smooth, and the chariot had not stopped until they arrived in Ifè. King Adéorí and Queen Adénìké were received by the Oòni and his *oloris* (queens). Although the hour was late, the palace had prepared a ceremonial welcome display for the great King of

Ìkirè Kingdom and his queen. A large crowd of people waited to welcome King Adéorí, who was well-known to the citizens of Ifè. As a part of the welcome, drummers played traditional talking drums, and dancers displayed their adept skills to entertain the King and the Queen. The energy from the singing and chanting of the crowd who had come out to welcome them was electrifying.

The welcome came as a pleasant surprise to King Adéorí since he hadn't expected any ceremony or crowds, considering the late hour. Queen Adénìké and everyone in the King's entourage was also very surprised but elated at the welcome. The Oòni and King Adéorí greeted one another in a warm and friendly manner, and the Oòni's olorìs also exchanged pleasantries with Adéorí and Adénìké. The monarchs and queens all watched the performances for a short while before the Oóni ushered King Adéorí and Queen Adénìké into his palace. The drummers and dancers continued playing until the crowd dispersed for the night.

While the Oòni and King Adéorí went ahead to the living room area, the two youngest of the Oòni's five queens—who were all about the same age as Queen Adénìké—took Adénìké to the royal residence where she and her husband would stay during their visit. The Oòni's palace was more modern than most palaces in the region. The Oòni was arguably the wealthiest monarch in the region, and his palace had been built with concrete and thoroughly polished wood and was very sophisticated. As the queens walked toward the royal residence with their maidens and escort guards, Queen Adénìké admired the beauty and grandeur of the palace. Adénìké, like many others, had heard so many stories about the Oòni's wealth and his beautiful palace, but upon seeing it with her own eyes, even in the dark, she decided it was much grander than expected.

Her husband was a regular visitor at the palace as the Oòni was seventy-eight years old and had been a close friend and ally of King Adéorí's father. The Oòni had ascended the throne at the age of twenty-four after his father, Oòni Olúwoyè, had passed. As a young boy, Adéorí had visited the Oòni's palace a few times with his father, and the relationship had continued to grow even after his own father's demise.

At the entrance to the royal residence, the Oòni's queens, Olorì Atinúké and Olori Abímbólá, led the way, and Queen Adéníké followed behind them with the maidens and the guards.

'Olorì Adéníké, we have prepared this place for you and his Majesty,' said Queen Atinúké, as they stepped into a large living area. 'We hope that you are pleased and will enjoy it during your stay with us.'

'Of course. This place is very beautiful,' Adéníké responded, glancing around.

Smiling, Queen Abímbólá added, 'We are glad you like it. We have been preparing for your visit for a few weeks, and it is our honour and desire to make sure you are comfortable. The other queens and I are also looking forward to learning more about you.'

'Thank you, Olorì Abímbólá. This is perfect, and yes, I am happy to be here. I am also looking forward to all the advantages that will result from this visit and getting to know everyone as well.'

'Wonderful! Let's take a look around to make sure you have everything you need,' said Abímbólá.

'Yes, of course,' agreed Adéníké. They walked around together. Queen Adéníké admired the residence, which consisted of a living area, two bedrooms, and three additional rooms for the maidens and the King's personal staff. 'This is just perfect. I am sure my husband will like it, too. It is also very calm and relaxing. Thank you, Olorì Atinúké and Abímbólá. You are welcome to visit us in the future as well, so we can reciprocate this kind gesture.'

'Yes, we will visit,' Queen Atinúké answered excitedly. 'We missed the final pankration tournament match this year. The pankration competition is a famous palace tradition in Ikire organized by the King's guards during the end of year harvest break where sixteen of the strongest palace servants contest in a unique mixture of full contact wrestling and boxing match. We should have been there, but Kábíyèsí had to attend an important meeting in the Northern region with some Northern leaders, and we were all required to go with him at the last minute, but we will not miss the next one. We know it is usually packed with fun.'

'You will have no excuse for missing the next one,' said Adénìké, laughing along with the other queens. While the queens chatted, the guards unloaded the chariot and brought in the luggage.

During a break in the conversation, Queen Atinúké told Adénìké, 'The Aláàfin and his wife, Olorì Bùkólá, are staying in the other residence in the next building. They arrived about two hours before you did. I am sure we will all have a nice time visiting tomorrow.'

Abímbólá and Adénìké both nodded. 'I am so looking forward to that. Thank you very much again,' responded Adénìké.

'We will take our leave now, Olorì, so you can get some rest after your long journey,' said Queen Abímbólá. 'If you require something to eat or drink or need anything whatsoever, the staff is at your service.'

'*Esé gan* (Thank you very much),' Adénìké replied.

'Good night, Adénìké,' said the Oòni's queens, as they withdrew with their guards from their guests' area of the royal residence.

Not long after they'd left, King Adéorí arrived at the residence escorted by his guards along with a few of the Oòni's guards. The guards prostrated themselves and uttered, 'Kábíyèsí o,' and the King discharged them of their duties for the night. King Adéorí waved his staff at them, thanked them all for their dedication, and entered the royal residence, where Queen Adénìké was waiting. The Oòni's guards returned to their quarters while King Adéorí's guards proceeded to the rooms made available for them behind the royal residence to spend the night.

Queen Adénìké had taken a warm bath and changed into comfortable clothing. She sat in the residence's living room with a cup of palm wine, waiting for her husband. King Adéorí walked in, looking quite tired after a very long day. 'Welcome back, *olówó orí mi* (the one who paid my dowry),' she said to the King.

'*Osé, olorì mi* (Thank you, my Queen),' he replied. He took off his crown, and she got up to help him remove his agbádá before he sat down in one of the chairs.

'You look very tired, my lord,' said Adénìké. 'Today has been a long day, and you were unable to rest before going into discussions with the Oòni. I know it is too late for you to eat a meal at this time, but would you like me to get you anything, my King? Olorìs Abímbólá and Atinúké have made many preparations to ensure our comfort and make us feel at home.'

'That was very kind of them. The Oòni has also been very nice, as usual,' Adéorí answered. 'The Aláàfin met us in the palace, and one discussion led to another. Bring me some water, and I will also have some palm wine with you, but water first, my dear.'

The Queen went to get some water for her husband as the King took off his sandals. She returned with a jug of water and a jar of palm wine as requested and knelt down to serve him.

'Thank you, my Queen. The sight of you excites me. Please, get up, my dear,' he said with a smile.

Queen Adénìké blushed as she poured him a second cup of water. 'You say the sweetest things, my lord,' said Adénìké, getting up to sit beside her husband.

King Adéorí filled each of their cups with more wine before speaking. 'I hope you are not missing home yet, Dénìké,' he teased.

'Not yet, my King,' she replied. 'You know that home is where I love to be, but I am also looking forward to meeting and spending time with the olorìs. The two I met today seemed very nice. I am so happy and honoured to have joined you on this trip, my King. I am thankful.'

'*Kò tópé* (You are welcome). I want you to be here with me, so it is my pleasure,' he said, touching Adénìké's cheek like he always did.

'By the way, my King, I have been wondering about something since you first asked me to join you—why did you decide to bring *me* with you on this very important trip instead of *ìyálé mi* (my older queen), who usually attends these types of meetings with you? Or Olorì Olúfúnké, who is younger and should be your favourite since she is presently pregnant with the heir to the throne?'

King Adéorí shook his head slowly while the Olorí waited for his response. '*Omodé ò mo ògùn óuń pè ní èfó* (A child who does not know a medicinal leaf will call it a vegetable),' he replied with a smile. 'You are my favourite, Dénìké. You know I always prefer to listen to my instincts and intuition. Our intuitions have great power. The meeting we are here to attend is important, not just for the other monarchs and me but for the entirety of the Yorùbá people. Everything I do and every decision I make before, during, and after the meeting must be in line with my intuition. *Ìwo ni ogbón inú mi yàn* (You are the one my intuition chose). That is why you are here with me. I know that you sometimes make a lot of mistakes and allow the things of the world to get in the way of your decision-making, but I see your heart better than you do, and I know it is pure.'

As she listened to her husband, Adénìké's heart skipped a beat, and she became worried and afraid. He definitely knew something he wasn't telling her yet. *Was there another motive behind his bringing her on this trip?* she wondered while the King took a long gulp from his cup of wine.

King Adéorí set his cup down and took a deep breath before he continued: 'My darling Dénìké, you look worried,' said the King. 'Please, don't be. Don't let my decision to bring you here with me bother you. All you need to know is that you are very special to me, my dear.

'The hour is very late, and we should get some sleep. Tomorrow will be a very busy day, too. The meeting begins tomorrow at ten.' He rose and kissed Olorì Adénìké on the forehead. 'Where is the room prepared for us?' he asked, smiling.

Adénìké smiled back as she led her husband to their room, but her thoughts continued to race. Before long, the King and Queen retired for the night.

SEVEN

---•◦•---

The night was short, and Friday morning broke very early at the Oòni's palace. As early as six, the palace staff moved around, cleaning and preparing for the day's occasion. More monarchs were expected to arrive at the palace that morning for the meeting, and additional guests were scheduled to arrive later in the day and on Saturday to join in for the weekend celebrations. Events at the Oòni's palace were famous for their extravagant nature, and the Oòni was known for sparing no expense in preparation. His queens were tasked with the duties of organizing such events and making sure that they did not fall short of expectations.

The staff finished most of the morning chores by eight. Various groups of entertainers who had been selected to perform—such as dancers, drummers, musicians, tricksters, and comedians—began to arrive and set up for the day. Some of the best painters, sculptors, and artists in Ifè Kingdom had also been invited to add some colour to the event by showcasing their work in the hope that some guests might also show interest in buying them. As the morning progressed, more people arrived, and the mood in the palace gradually transformed into a festive one.

According to the agenda, the monarchs were to have breakfast together at nine before the meeting commenced at ten. Just before nine, the Aláké of Ègbá, one of three monarchs who hadn't arrived the previous day, reached the palace with his olorì and entourage. The Aláké received a warm reception at the entrance and was ushered into the palace by the guards. The other monarchs had settled in and were about to begin breakfast when the Aláké walked in with his olorì. The monarchs exchanged pleasantries, and the breakfast routine began.

Thirty minutes later, the arrival of the Oba of Benin, the Awùjalè of Ìjèbú, and the British businessmen were announced, and they were all ushered directly to a waiting room adjacent to the Oòni's private meeting room. The Oòni and the other three monarchs left the dining hall as soon as they finished breakfast and proceeded together to the meeting area. Another round of greetings and pleasantries ensued as the monarchs and visitors converged in the waiting room before the Oòni led them into his private meeting room, and the doors were closed behind them.

The monarchs and the British visitors were quickly seated in the beautifully designed and furnished meeting room. Once everyone had settled without delay, the Oòni opened the meeting with a short introductory speech. Following his speech, the spokesperson for the group of British businessmen stood up to address the monarchs. He explained their proposal and intentions in detail and outlined how their partnership would bring benefits both to their company and to the people of the Yorùbá land.

Due to the recent rise in demand for chocolate and beverages whose primary, raw material was the cocoa widely grown in the region, the British businessmen were keen on creating partnerships that would give them sole trade and procurement rights. The region arguably boasted the most fertile land for the cultivation of cocoa, and gaining sole trade rights would give the company a considerable competitive advantage over other global competitors. The men representing their company's interests understood the importance of exercising the first-mover advantage and sealing the agreement with the region. They had also taken advantage of the great relationship their company had built with the Oòni over the years by bringing other monarchs in the region together for a meeting in which they would, hopefully, achieve a general consensus. The strategy was more effective than meeting with the monarchs individually and trying to negotiate several different partnership agreements. According to the spokesman's proposal, the British company would pay a one-time fee for owning the sole purchase rights of the raw materials and consequently pay a premium for the raw materials as they were procured for export from the region. For many of the monarchs present, this sounded like a very good deal as they would be receiving more than the average profit they typically made from the sale of a ton of cocoa. Some of the monarchs obviously appeared ready to accept the proposed offer from the British businessmen.

Once the spokesman finished his presentation, the Oòni called on King Adéorí to address the monarchs and the businessmen and give them his impression of how the agreement negotiations should proceed. The close relationship between the Oòni and

King Adéorí wasn't a surprise to the other monarchs. More often than not, King Adéorí's business acumen had proven to be highly beneficial in negotiations, and the monarchs knew how important it was to hear his point of view before making a decision on the partnership.

King Adéorí cleared his throat and began his address: '*Modúpé modè tún júbà Olódùmarè, asèdá ayé, asèdá òrun* (I give thanks, and I salute God Almighty, the creator of the earth and the creator of the heavens)—the reason we were here yesterday and are here today and by his mercy, we will be here tomorrow. I salute the gods of our precious land and our ancestors. Our people say that *àgbà kí wà ní ojà kí orí omo tuntun ó wó* (an infant's head cannot be bent over while an elder is present in the market). I use this opportunity to call on our ancestors and elders to guide us in the right direction so we can make the best decision for our land, our children, and our future generations.'

The other monarchs called out, 'Àse,' in agreement.

Adéorí continued. 'I greet my mentor, the Oòni, for making this event possible. I also greet the Aláàfin, the Oba of great Benin, the Aláké, and Awùjalè for your presence today. Our collective commitment to our land and our people will yield us the best results by the power of Olódùmarè.'

'Àse,' echoed the monarchs.

'I also greet our visitors from Great Britain today,' said the King, 'and I welcome you again on behalf of me, my fellow monarchs, and the people of our land. Without taking too much of our time, I will immediately address the reason why we are all here.

'I strongly believe that what makes a partnership agreement successful is for both sides to contribute something tangible to the partnership as well as receive something tangible out of the partnership. The only way this is possible is for both parties involved to fully understand the value of what they are giving and getting as well as the value of what the other party is giving and getting in return. This understanding is very important, especially in long-term business arrangements, because as time passes, both parties should continue to be comfortable with the decision they have made at the onset of the agreement in order to foster a seamless and productive working relationship together.

'In addition, I think it is safe and significant to point out that our land produces the best variety of cocoa that can be found anywhere in the world. Our soil is so fertile that merely dropping a seed on the ground without expending any extra effort, the seed will grow and germinate. Our cocoa is used to produce the premium chocolates and beverages that are currently in high demand throughout Europe and America, and I am sure our visitors can confirm that this current demand isn't anywhere near its peak yet. To add to that, I am sure our contemporaries from Britain would not be able to tell us how much profit their company will generate per ton of cocoa they purchase from us,' he said, smiling as he looked at each British businessman, all of whom were giving him their full attention.

'In fact, I am sure they would agree that they will make a great deal of money, and without our high-yielding land and labour, these huge profits wouldn't be achievable. Of course, we realize that our partners might have other options to source their raw materials, but we also know that our partners understand *we* are the best option for them. Hence, the reason they have come to us first before their competitors in Europe and other parts of the world,' added the King, continuing to smile warmly while focusing his attention on the visitors. The other monarchs listened patiently, knowing that everything King Adeori said was absolutely true.

'Taking all that has been said into account, I want to thank our partners for their proposal. We will accept the large advance payments for each monarch's region. We will also accept the premium price for our cocoa, which, in my opinion, sounds more like the right price. In addition, I propose that our partners also commit to building both primary and secondary schools in regions controlled by the monarchs present here today. Furthermore, our partners will also commit to building hospitals and health centres in all regions in which they conduct business. The schools and hospitals must be built to standard, and our partners must also properly equip these facilities and fund their operations throughout the duration of the agreement. At the end of the duration of our agreement, our partners will return the operations of these facilities to us. Prior to that time, some of our own people will have been properly trained on how to maintain these facilities so we can continue to properly maintain them ourselves.'

King Adéorí paused and took a long drink from the cup of water on the table. The Oòni's meeting room was silent. The monarchs nodded their heads in acceptance, their expressions mirroring his gesture. They were very impressed with the King's speech as his proposal considered the progress of the entirety of the Yorùbá land and its people.

Adéorí set down his cup and cleared his throat. 'Finally, I would like to reassure our partners that we will do everything within our power to ensure that our part of the agreement is fulfilled, and their company will have access to our cocoa and efficient labour to the optimum advantage of the business. We want you to know that when you win, we win, and vice versa.

'I hope I have spoken well for my fellow monarchs and our people. I also hope our partners who are present fully understand our wishes as presented in this proposal. Lest I forget, we welcome any recommendations for *additional* social responsibilities your company would like to include in the proposal for the progress of our communities,' he added good-naturedly but with some seriousness.

The monarchs and the British businessmen laughed at the last comment as King Adéorí wrapped up his speech. 'I thank you all, most especially the Oòni, who has made this meeting possible. I pray that Olódùmarè and the gods of our land guide our steps in all our actions today and in the future to come.'

In unison, the monarchs said, 'Àse!'

After King Adéorí's speech, some of the monarchs whispered to one another while the British businessmen talked amongst themselves in low voices. These conversations went on for several minutes before the Oòni spoke up: 'Thank you, Oba Adéorí. You have spoken exceptionally well, as always. I propose we take a fifteen-minute break for some refreshments,' he said, pointing at the large pendulum clock on the wall, 'after which we will continue the meeting, and the Aláàfin will speak to the group.'

The Oòni's private meeting room was very large and spacious and divided into a few beautifully designed and furnished sections. The monarchs and the businessmen had gathered around a rectangular, wooden table and sat in upright yet comfortable chairs. This area was well lit by the many torches set in bronze torch stands surrounding the table. After the Oòni had called for a short break, some of the monarchs moved to another section of the room. The luxurious wooden chairs in that section had obviously been designed for relaxation. A jar of wine was on a table in a corner along with some fruit and kolanut for refreshment and lanterns for soft lighting. Another section of the room was beautifully decorated with artefacts, sculptures, and precious stones that told unique stories about Ifé Kingdom and its former rulers. The British businessmen were attracted to that section of the room, and they moved from one piece of artwork to the next, closely examining and admiring each piece. A few of them had visited the Oòni's palace in the past, but they had never set foot in the private meeting room. Every part of the palace was unique, and the British guests were amazed at the level of detail and beauty of the pieces on display.

The men broke into different groups within the meeting room, and three of the Oòni's palace staff were granted access into the room to serve more wine. King Adéorí settled into one of the more luxurious chairs and was served some fruit and wine by one of the palace staff.

The Aláké came around and eased into the chair on his right. A younger man in his early forties, the Aláké had only recently ascended the throne of Ègbáland after his late father had passed away four years ago. He was fast becoming a force with which to be reckoned in the entire region because of his success at improving business relationships by a hundred-fold during his reign. His kingdom and people were also quickly becoming wealthier than the inhabitants of other parts of the Yorùbá land due to the opportunities his business relationships created for them. The young Aláké's patience and respect for all monarchs, even those whose territorial control was smaller than his, had earned him favour amongst older monarchs in the region and beyond.

Once the Aláké had sat down, a staff member approached him to offer more wine. 'Some wine and kolanut,' requested the Aláké. He got comfortable in the seat next to King Adéorí before initiating a conversation: '*Ekú ìjókò, Oba Adéorí* (Happy sitting, King Adéorí).'

'Thank you, Oba Adédàmólá. It is good to see you,' replied Adéorí.

'Likewise. It is a great pleasure to be in your midst today and in the midst of other great rulers of our land. I have heard so many wonderful things about you.'

'Thank you for the compliments, Aláké. I have heard about the good things you have done in Ègbá, as well. I pray Olódùmarè gives us all the strength to do what is right for our people.'

'Àse, Oba,' agreed Aláké. 'Much of the thanks goes to you, Oba Adéorí. I want to use this opportunity to thank you for your support, especially during the past two years. We would not be able to do many of the things we do without the support we receive from your kingdom.'

King Adéorí wondered about the Aláké's last comment. He could not recall having given the Aláké or any delegate from Ègbá any form of support in recent times. Forgetting about his dealings with other monarchs was quite unusual for King Adéorí, but after thinking about it for a few moments, he concluded that he must have rendered them some form of support, even if he could not remember it now.

'I should have visited you myself to thank you for everything,' continued Aláké, 'but your delegates that have been coming to Ègbá to represent your interests tell me how busy you have been, so we concluded they would inform us about the best time to visit you.'

King Adéorí sensed something was going on that he didn't know about. Forgetting that delegates from Ìkirè had visited the Aláké for something as important as he portrayed would be impossible, but on the remote chance he had forgotten something, he decided to play along. 'Yes, I have been quite busy, but now, please accept my official invitation, Oba Adédàmólá. Just notify us a fortnight prior to your visit, and we will make plans. You should also bring the olorì and spend a couple of nights with us if you wish.

'That is so generous of you, Oba Adéorí,' said Adédàmólá. 'We will surely visit. I know she will be excited about that. I would also like to invite you to the opening ceremony for some of the major roads we have newly constructed in Ègbá. I didn't want to pass the message through your delegates, but after seeing you here, I thought this occasion was perfect for inviting you in person. These roads are the largest constructed in Ègbá, and the money for the project came by way of our dealings with your kingdom, Oba Adéorí. My council of elders and I have decided we want you to commission the roads because, without you, this wouldn't have been achievable in the time it took to complete.'

At that point, King Adéorí was totally perplexed. It was evident that something of which he had no knowledge had occurred. The Aláké was a smart man, and Adéorí didn't want to give him the impression that he was unaware of whatever that was. As he contemplated how to respond, the Oòni raised his voice to inform everyone present that it was time to resume the meeting.

'Thank you, Oba Adédàmólá,' Adéorí said hastily. 'It would be an honour to do so, and I will keep that in mind. I look forward to receiving the official invitation and to your future visit to my palace. We must return to the meeting now.' He stood up, and the Aláké did the same. Both monarchs walked back to the large, central table to rejoin the others for the meeting.

EIGHT

—————•❖•—————

The second half of the meeting started with the Aláàfin's speech, followed by the other monarchs, who took turns sharing their opinions and views of the partnership. After all the monarchs had a chance to speak, they came to a consensus about King Adéorí's proposal for the partnership because it encapsulated what every one of the monarchs wanted from the partnership plus much more. The monarchs then spoke for another hour, after which the seven British businessmen congregated to deliberate over everything they had heard. These businessmen were key figures who represented their company and had the power to make decisions on its behalf as long as they were harmonious.

After about fifteen minutes of discussion amongst themselves, the visitors' spokesman briefly addressed the monarchs to confirm they had concluded to proceed with King Adéorí's proposal. The monarchs were delighted with the outcome. The British partners were also very happy, not only because they would benefit tremendously from the deal and make huge profits from the added value to the raw cocoa, but because they had received the full support of the monarchs, which was very important to them. Of course, they were accustomed to dealing with monarchs in the region who would accept their proposals without any opposition. Yet, when they listened to King Adéorí's speech, it had become clear that these negotiations would be different. King Adéorí obviously had knowledge of their business and was determined to get the best out of the deal for his people.

Finally, the time had come to conclude the proceedings. The monarchs and businessmen all signed an initial memorandum of understanding to demonstrate the full interest of both sides in the partnership and that a new deal had been established. The Oòni called in his staff to serve them all another cup of wine to toast to the new partnership. Monarchs and businessmen alike raised their cups for the toast and joyfully finished off their wine. They got up from the table and followed the Oòni out of the meeting room, ready to join the celebrations that kicked off with some singing and dancing.

This agenda of continuous events meant the celebration would hold plenty of fun with abundant food and beverages for everyone. The performers thrilled the guests, and the cheering from the on-looking crowd was unceasing, with hardly a moment of silence throughout. The celebrations lived up to the expectations for a typical Oòni event. A few hours later, the palace was still filled with guests and people from Ifè Kingdom who all thoroughly enjoyed the festivities.

The British businessmen were the first of the main guests to take their leave. They were travelling back to Lagos that evening so they could have some time to relax before their journey back to Britain in a couple of days. The Oòni, the Aláàfin, King Adéorí, and an entourage of guards walked the British men to their vehicle. The businessmen promised to deliver the final piece of paperwork for signing to all of the monarchs in six weeks' time. Once all of the paperwork was signed and returned, the British company would begin construction of the three facilities for the processing of raw materials before they were transported to Britain for the final phases of value addition. It was projected that the facilities would be completed within six months in strategic locations. Presently, Ìkirè, Ìbàdàn, and Ègbá were being considered.

The spokesman for the British company, who had recently met King Adéorí for the first time, was intrigued after listening to his speech, and he promised to visit the King at his palace on his next trip back to the region. The men exchanged their final greetings. The monarchs wished the men well, and the British businessmen thanked the Oòni for his kind hospitality before hopping into the chariot. The monarchs watched as the vehicle drove away before proceeding back to join the others in the celebration.

As they walked back to the palace, King Adéorí informed the Oòni and Aláàfin that he would also be leaving soon. Initially, King Adéorí's plan had been to stay at the Oòni's palace until Saturday, but he had changed his mind and told Olorì Adénìké about his decision to return to his palace that evening.

Adénìké had enjoyed meeting the other queens, and they had planned to spend the evening together after the celebration. She had anticipated spending more time with the other queens, but her husband had made up his mind to leave without giving her any reason for it. She wondered what could have prompted his abrupt decision but decided not to bother herself with the situation. His wish was her command, after all. While King Adéorí chatted and strolled back with the other monarchs to the celebration, as a courtesy, she went ahead to inform the other queens they would be leaving soon.

The Oòni had also thought King Adéorí would be spending the night at his palace. 'Oba Adéorí, my expectation was that you would leave for Ìkirè tomorrow. You seem to have changed your mind. *Sé kò sí* (I hope there is no problem),' he said.

'All is well, Oòni,' Adéorí assured him. 'You know I always love spending time here with you. I remembered that I had scheduled an engagement with Jagun, my chief of defence, and his men for tomorrow. One of my accompanying staff reminded me about it this afternoon. I had totally forgotten about it, but it is important I hold this meeting with them, Oòni.'

'Oh, that is fair enough,' replied the Oòni. 'Issues of security are very important and must be taken care of promptly. We monarchs usually have too many things on our minds and can easily forget some of these meetings. It is even worse for old men like the Aláàfin and me.' The three monarchs laughed.

'Oòni, I am still a young man,' protested the Aláàfin. 'So, I denounce being placed in that category,' he joked with a smile. 'We were expecting you to spend more time with us here, Oba Adéorí. You know we enjoy your company whenever we're able.'

King Adéorí responded, 'Yes, Aláàfin, I am sure we will do this again sometime soon. I am always very happy to be in the company of the two greatest men I know. I consider you both as father figures.'

'You are a strong leader and a great man yourself, Adéorí,' added the Oòni. 'We achieved a lot with you today. We would not have emerged with such a good deal without your participation.

We all cherish and appreciate your contribution and dedication to our land.'

'I second that,' said the Aláàfin.

'Thank you. I am glad. It is my duty and obligation to our land. I am flattered,' said Adéorí.

The monarchs arrived back at the celebration, and King Adéorí found Adénìké talking with the other queens, exchanging hugs and vows to visit one another in the future. He signalled to her that he was ready, and they both said their goodbyes to the monarchs one after the other before taking their leave. The servants and maidens had gathered to pack their belongings from the Oòni's palace residence and were waiting outside. The personal guards carrying the King's staff led the way as they prepared for the King and queen's entry into the waiting chariot. As soon as Adéorí and Adénìké were settled in, the personal guards boarded the second chariot, and the armed guards drove the chariots towards the gate leading out of the Oòni's palace.

Palace workers waved at the entourage as they exited, and the farewell continued as villagers and other onlookers waved at the departing chariot proceeding slowly through Ifè villages on their way back to Ìkirè. Shortly after the journey started and King Adéorí and Queen Adénìké stopped waving at those bidding them farewell, the King asked his wife to hand him the jar of water in the pouch beside her.

'*Ekú isé èní, oko mí* (Well done today, my husband). I am sure you must be very tired,' Queen Adénìké said as she passed the water to the King. He drank from the jar of water, took a deep breath, and exhaled a sigh of relief.

'*Osé, aya mí* (Thank you, my wife),' said Adéorí. 'Today was, indeed, a long day, but it was worth it. The meeting was a success. We were able to reach a solid agreement with our British partners, one that will go a long way toward benefiting our people tremendously. One highlight of the agreement involves the new schools and health centres that will be built in the region, and there will be a new school and health centre in Ìkirè for our people, too.'

'That is so wonderful, my lord!' she said. 'Health and education are paramount for the growth of our people. I am sure they will be excited once this new development begins.'

'I believe so, too,' King Adéorí replied with a tired smile. 'I hope you had a good time engaging with the other olorìs?'

'Yes, my lord,' said the Queen. 'I am very pleased to have come along with you on this trip. The olorìs are all very nice. We have agreed to keep in touch, and we are considering starting some type of collective work for our people, perhaps a foundation that will help all citizens across the region, but especially the less privileged, young women, and children. I am excited about that.'

'That sounds very promising. I am certain the other monarchs will readily support such a foundation. This is an auspicious time for our region because most of us are on the same page when it comes to issues concerning our people and moving them forward towards better times and better lives.'

She nodded her acceptance and hugged her husband. Just listening to him and spending time with him gave her so much joy. 'Amongst all of the queens, I bonded the most with Oba Adédàmólá's wife, Moréniké. She is only two years older than me, and we realized very early in our conversation that we have a lot in common. She talked about how much her husband speaks of Your Majesty and how you have been instrumental in Ègbá's fast progress. I couldn't respond much about that because I don't know of your business dealings with Oba Adédàmólá, but I appreciated all of her nice comments on your behalf.' Adénìké paused, smiling radiantly. 'She also mentioned something about her husband planning to visit you at the palace and inviting you to an event in Ègbáland sometime soon.'

As Adénìké narrated the details of her conversation with Olorì Moréniké, King Adéorí compared them with the conversation he'd had with the Aláké earlier, during the short break in the meeting. His brief discussion with the Aláké had been the reason for King Adéorí's change of mind and his decision to leave the Oòni's palace today instead of tomorrow as planned. He disliked being caught unawares, and discovering hidden information meant a lot to him, no matter how minute. Obviously, the information gleaned from the exchange with the Aláké was not minor, and the situation required immediate investigation. King Adéorí knew it was vital, and Adénìké's conversation with Olorì Moréniké confirmed it.

Since he understood nothing about the information or the business dealings that seemed to be important to the Aláké and his land, the King's first move would be to return to his palace— the safest place for him—and begin looking into the situation immediately. He listened to Adénìké without disclosing any of his thoughts on the matter or mentioning his conversation with the Aláké. At that moment, finding out who was behind the deals with the Aláké and his people was most important to King Adéorí. Who could have been using his name under the guise that they'd received orders to conduct business on his behalf? What if this was also happening elsewhere?

These questions briefly distracted him from what Adénìké was saying. After a few moments, the King refocused his attention on theQueen, who had stopped speaking long enough to open the food pouch and take out some *dòdò Ìkirè* (Ìkirè plantain bites) to snack on.

'My lord,' continued the Queen, 'the only thing that baffled me about what Olorì Moréniké said was that she had been sending gifts to us through the people from our kingdom who have been visiting on Your Majesty's behalf. She mentioned specifically sending gift items through one Agboolá and Bólájókò on two different occasions. I could not tell her that I had not received anything from her since it was likely the gifts must have been given to my ìyálé, Queen Adéòsun.' Adénìké looked at her husband, expecting a response.

The names Agboolà and Bólájókò were instantly familiar to King Adéorí. These two men from Òsógbo had been brought in to propose a deal to his council about a year and a half prior. He remembered that their proposal had been denied because it wasn't well-grounded, but he couldn't remember any of the details. He vaguely remembered that Queen Adéòsun had spoken to him a few times about their proposal. Adéòsun rarely got involved in the business of the kingdom, but at that time, she tried to convince him their proposal would be worth it. Her involvement had been absolutely welcome, and while he had commended her for sharing her thoughts on the proposal, he had also explained why it could not be accepted.

King Adéorí smiled as the chariot rocked gently on the journey back to the palace. Adénìké had just unknowingly provided an important piece of the puzzle: two names with which to begin his investigations. He knew a higher power must be involved with orchestrating whatever scheme these men were a part of, and he vowed to himself to get to the root of it all. Who could be behind this? Who could be carrying out these business dealings in his name, using the wealth and resources of his land and generating huge proceeds without his consent?

A kìí bá oba pàlà kí okó oba má sàn ni lésè (One does not share a farm boundary with a king without getting one's feet gashed by the king's hoe). In other words, one should be cautious in dealing with people in authority.

The story has begun, but the story will continue.

GLOSSARY

---◦•◦---

Ìkirè Kingdom, lower Guinea Region, Africa: southern region of modern-day Nigeria

Yorùbá – English

a kìí fá orí léyìn olórí – we can't shave a head in the absence of the owner

a kìí bá oba pàlà kí okó oba má sań ni lésè – one does not share a farm boundary with a king without getting one's feet gashed by the king's hoe

a kòle rí inú eni torí inú ènìyàn jìnà – we cannot see what is inside a person because the inside of a person is very far away

àbúrò – younger sibling

adé – crown

àdìre ìró àti bùbá – tie and dye wrapper and blouse

àgbà kí wà ní ojà kí orí omo tuntun ó wó – an infant's head cannot be bent over while an elder is present in the market

agbádá – long flowing robe with wide sleeves

agbára sùúrù kò sé fi ojú di nígbà ìsoro – the power of patience can never be underestimated in times of crisis and confusion

agbenu òrìsà ńlá – mouthpiece of the gods

Ahón re mú ní ìròlé yì – your tongue is sharp this evening

Arìwá – Northern region

àse – amen

àse, oba – Amen, my King

àse, olúwa mi – Amen, my lord

àtipé miò tì rí ńkàn osù mi – and I haven't seen my period

àwon èyan wà so wípé tí àgbàlagbà bá rí nkan tó ru lójú, ojú náà ni a fín wò se – our people say that if an elder sees something that is unpleasant, it is the same eyes that he will use to see it in order to amend it

aya oba – wife of a king

ayò mí tidé o, ayò mí tidé – my joy has arrived, my happiness has arrived

bàá mi – my father

bámi bí o, óti gbà lówó mi – ask him for me, he has taken her from me

béèni bàá mi – yes, my father

béèni Oko mí, orun alááfia ni mo sùn – yes, my husband, my sleep was peaceful bí omo adìe tó ń tèlé ìya rè kiri – like a chick following the mother hen everywhere

dáada ni mo wà – I am doing very well

dìde ńlè – rise from the floor

dòdò Ìkirè – Ìkirè plantain bites

dùndún – fried sweet cocoyam

ègbón mi – my older brother

ekáarò olorì àgbà – good morning, older queen

ekáàsán oko mí – good afternoon, my husband

èko – cornmeal

ekú àárò, oko mí – good morning, my husband

ekú alé bàá mi – good evening my father

ekú árò o – good morning

ekú ìjókò – happy sitting

ekú isé èní oko mí – well done today, my husband

ekú isé o – work well done

elèdá mi mo dúpé o – thank you, my creator

èmi náà se àdéhùn fún bàbá mi wípé mà ná owó mà sí nà ára láti ri pé a borí – I also promised my father that I will spend my money, my body, and everything within my power to see that we win this battle

eni tí ń so òru dì árò – the one that turns the night into day epo pupa – palm oil

esé – thank you

esé gan – thank you very much

esé tí e jí mi sí orí lè ayé lénì yí – thank you for waking me up on the earth today

etí méjì míràn kò gbodò báwa gbó nkan tí a sè o – another pair of ears must not hear what we have cooked up

etí re kòní le gbà – your ears wouldn't have been able to hear without getting hurt

èwà àti isu dídín – beans and fried yam

èwò – abomination

filà – cap

ibà – fever

ifura ni ògùn àgbà – the greatest weapon of the elders is suspicion

ìkìlò – warning

inílò àwon ará ìlú níse àkókó, kí ti wa tó tèle – the needs of the people come first, before ours can follow

inú mi dùn ayò mí kún – I am so happy and full of joy

ìró – wrapper: piece of cloth that women tie around their waists

iwo ni ogbón inú mi yàn – you are the one my intuition chose

iyálé mi – my older queen; the wife before me; my older wives

iyàwó mi – the wife after me

kìí se mímò mi, esé o – it's not of my own doing, thank you

kó má bà sí ni o fi rí mi olorì Adénìké – it is so no problems will
arise, that is why I am here, Queen Adénìké

kò sí eni tín bèrè bí ase kó orò jo; orò ni orò ń jé – nobody asks
how wealth is acquired; wealth is wealth

kò tópé – no need to thank me; you are welcome

kòsí eni kéni tí a bí láti inú obìrin tí yìò gbó nkan tí a sè láti enu mí
– no person born from a woman will hear what we have
cooked up from me

kù àárò, aya mí, aya oba – good morning, my wife, the wife of the
King

láì pé – very soon

láti èní lo títí láilái ayò mí tidé o – from today onwards and forever
more, my joy has arrived

lénu ojó méta – for the past three days

màámi ńkó – how about our mother

mábìnú sí mi òré mi – don't be upset with me, my friend

mo jú bà a sè èdá ayé – I salute you, the creator of the world

mo jú bà àwon Irúnmolè – I salute the deities of our land

mo jú bà Olódùmarè – I salute you oh Lord

mo jú bà Olórun mí àti Olórun àwon baba mi – I salute you my
lord and the lord of my forefathers

mo lè je ilé pèlú irú ebi tó ńpa mí yì – I could eat a house with the type of hunger I feel right now

modúpé modè tún júbà Olódùmarè, asèdá ayé, asèdá òrun – I give thanks, and I salute God Almighty, the creator of the earth and the creator of the heavens

moi moi – steamed bean pudding

ní agbára Olódùmarè olorì àgbà – by the grace of the Almighty, older queen

nkan tó bá kan ójú yí ò padà kan ímú – whatever affects the eye will eventually affect the nose

nkan tó n se Adénìké jù béèlo – what is wrong with Adénìké is more than that

ó dá mi lójú wípé inú bàbá mi yí ò dùn – I am sure my father would be happy

o káre Àlàbí, gbé ra ńlè – well done Àlàbí, get up

o seun – thank you

ó yán si mí létí lénu ojó méta yì pé ó seése kí Adénìké ti férakù – it has come to my knowledge these past few days that Adénìkè is likely pregnant

oba àwon sòrò sòrò – king of the talkative

oba gbo gbo, aláyélúwà – king of all, the omniscient

oba kìí subú bí ó wà láyé àbí kò sí láyé – a king doesn't fall whether he is alive or dead oba nígbà ayé, oba lójú orun – a king while on earth and a king in death

ode – security men or vigilantes

okáre, omo mí, omo olá, àjí rí dunnú – well done, my child, a child born in wealth, one who brings you joy when you set your eyes on her in the morning after waking up

oko mí – my husband

Oláolú fé kó bá mi – Oláolú wants to put me in trouble

Olódùmarè ní fun ni lómo – It is the Almighty that gives a child

olólùfé mi, oko mí, olówó orí mi – my lover, my husband, and the owner of my dowry

olówó orí mi – the one who paid my dowry

olówó orí mi, oko mi, olólùfé mi, eni okàn mí yàn – the one who paid my dowry, my husband, my lover, the one my heart chooses and desires

omo tí a kó tó gbèkó – a child whom we taught and who also allowed herself to be taught

omodé ò mo ògùn óuń pè ní èfó – a child who does not know a medicinal leaf will call it a vegetable

orí adé – the crown

òrò tí a kò fé kí baba ó gbó, baba ní ó parí rè – the issue we don't want father to know about, the same father will help to resolve osé aya mi – thank you, my wife

óse é se pé mo ti férakù – it is possible that I am pregnant

osé, olorì mi – thank you, my queen

rárá o olówó orí mi – not at all my husband

àbúrò mí tòótó, báwo ni gbogbo nkan – my sincere younger sister,
how is everything

sé dada lo jí – I hope you woke up well

sé kò sí – I hope there is no problem

sé ò sí – I hope there is no problem

shé àlááfìà ni àwon naá wà – I hope she is also doing well

sòkòtò – trousers

sùgbón ìkìlò kán wà – but there is a warning

tí a bá sì ma finú han eni, kòsí eni tí ó dàbi awo àti èjè eni – and if
we want to open up and show someone what's inside us,
no one is like one's own flesh and blood

wo lé o – come in

ABOUT THE AUTHOR

Babatunde Olaniran is extremely passionate about people and the progress of humanity as a whole. An only child who grew up in a large household with cousins and relatives, he attended the most prestigious high school in Nigeria, King's College Lagos. He holds a diploma in electrical and electronics engineering, a Bachelor of Technology in project management technology, an MBA, and a PMP certification. A native of Osun State, Nigeria, he was born and grew up in Lagos State, Nigeria, before moving to San Francisco, California in his late twenties. Babatunde is very passionate about food production and technology and worked at his family's agricultural food-processing business before earning an MBA degree in business at Hult International Business School in San Francisco, California, USA. He is a director and partner at Blakbloid Integrated Investment Limited (BiiLGroup), a Nigerian investment company that manages businesses in agriculture, logistics, automobiles, and technology. He enjoys reading just about anything, writing, and is famous for dishing out his opinions on his website, www.olaniran.com and YouTube channel 'Video Counsel'. This is his second book in the series, *Tales of an African Dynasty*. He also enjoys football, running, and taking long walks. Babatunde currently resides in Miami Beach, Florida and also has a home in Lagos, Nigeria, where he often loves to spend time visiting family and friends.

Other Books by Babatunde Olaniran

Unseen Depths of the Heart:
Tales of an African Dynasty (Book 1)

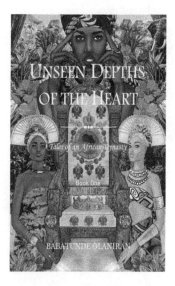

In the quest for an heir to the throne of Ikire Kingdom, supernatural powers are consulted even as lust reigns over prudence and deceit becomes an adopted way of life. Power and prosperity exude from King Adeori, whose lineage and ancestors have ruled the Kingdom for many centuries.

But the sins of ancestors are revealed and threaten to end the dynasty's reign of more than half a millennium. As every successful King needs the unwavering support of his Queen, only Adeori's Queens hold the key to finding the silver lining in this unprecedented dark cloud. Will they help breathe life into this great Kingdom or not? Only time will tell.

As the levels of treachery run deep in the autocratic powers and remain hidden to the naked eye, deploying innate wisdom and the visions of their inner consciousness is paramount for the King and his council before the situation becomes irreparable.

This powerful and captivating story promises to take you on an extraordinary ride that explores ancient and modern Yoruba literature as well as one of the first African traditions that still exist today and will remain for centuries to come.

Unseen Depths of the Heart is the first book in the series "Tales of an African Dynasty" This creative work of literature, storytelling and art promises to take you on an extraordinary ride that explores ancient and modern Yoruba literature as well as one of the first African traditions that still exist today and will remain for centuries to come.

Guaranteed to entertain, educate and captivate. An amazing read for travelers, story lovers, African tradition (Yoruba) enthusiasts and anyone who enjoys a great read.

Coming Soon

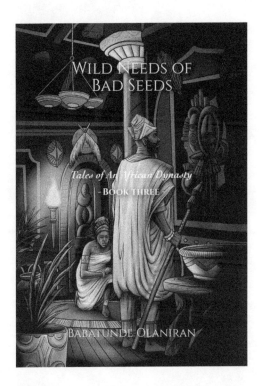

Connect with the Author

For more information, visit or contact
instagram: babatundeolaniran_
email: babs_olaniran@yahoo.com

CPSIA information can be obtained
at www.ICGtesting.com
Printed in the USA
BVHW041034061222
653555BV00004B/40